ST/ESA/PAD/SER.E/116

Department of Economic and Social Affairs
Division for Public Administration and
Development Management

Implementing the Millennium Development Goals: Challenges and Responses for Public Administration

Contribution of the United Nations Committee of Experts on Public Administration

Edited by:
Guido Bertucci
Allan Rosenbaum

United Nations
New York, 2007

Mission Statement

The Department of Economic and Social Affairs of the United Nations Secretariat is a vital interface between global policies in the economic, social and environmental spheres and national action. The Department works in three main interlinked areas: (i) it compiles, generates and analyses a wide range of economic, social and environmental data and information on which Member States of the United Nations draw to review common problems and to take stock of policy options; (ii) it facilitates the negotiations of Member States in many intergovernmental bodies on joint courses of action to address ongoing or emerging global challenges; and (iii) it advises interested Governments on the ways and means of translating policy frameworks developed in United Nations conferences and summits into programmes at the country level and, through technical assistance, helps build national capacities.

Notes

The designations employed and the presentation of the material in this publication do not imply the expression of any opinion whatsoever on the part of the Secretariat of the United Nations concerning the legal status of any country, territory, city or area, or of its authorities, or concerning the delimitation of its frontiers or boundaries.

The views expressed are those of the individual authors and do not imply any expression of opinion on the part of the United Nations.

Enquiries concerning this publication may be directed to:
Mr. Guido Bertucci
Director, Division for Public Administration and
Development Management, Department of Economic and Social Affairs
United Nations, New York, NY 10017, USA
Fax: (212)963-9681 Email:bertucci@un.org

ST/ESA/PAD/SER.E/116
United Nations publication
Sales No: E.08.II.H.3
ISBN 978-92-1-123175-5
Printed by the United Nations, New York

UN2
ST/ESA/PAD/SER.E/116

Foreword and Acknowledgements

The establishment of the Millennium Development Goals represents one of the most important and ambitious undertakings by the United Nations. As numerous studies have found, over one billion people currently live on less than one dollar a day. One of the principal objectives of the Millennium Development Goals is to, by the year 2015, cut this number in half. Obviously, the achievement of such a goal is at one and the same time both very important and not an easy task.

The Division of Public Administration and Development Management of the Department of Economic and Social Affairs of the United Nations is, as its name suggests, committed to helping countries, especially those in either economic or political transition, improve the quality of their governance through the support of both administrative and governance reform processes. This volume is part of the effort by the Division of Public Administration and Development Management to support the very important initiative represented by the Millennium Development Goals.

The papers that follow build upon two important activities of the Division. In so doing, they represent an effort to better understand the means by which the Millennium Development Goals can be achieved. These two activities include, first, the efforts of the Division to encourage and support the redefinition of government in such a manner as to make it a more effective instrument for the achievement of effective public policy. One part of this effort has been the organizing of a series of world-wide conferences concerned with the reinventing of government in such a manner as to make it both more effective and more responsive. As part of the preparation for the most recent Global Forum on the Reinventing Government, which focused on the issue of building trust in government, the Division supported the preparation of various reports which made significant contributions towards exploring the manner in which public policy that encouraged the achievement of the Millennium Development Goals could be developed.

The papers that follow go beyond the Division's work in the redefinition of government and carry that work to the next step. They are the product of yet another activity of the Division and that is the support to the Committee of Experts on Public Administration which has been established by the Economic and Social Council of the United Nations. This Committee brings together some of the most eminent experts – both practitioners and academics – in the field of public administration to address vital issues confronting governments throughout the world.

While attention has been focused on the need for effective public policy if the Millennium Development Goals are to be met, there is also the need to implement that public policy in such a manner that its objectives are actually achieved. This is because the achievement of any set of policy goals, and especially any as ambitious as the Millennium Development Goals, requires more than just good public policy. It requires the effective implementation of that policy and it is that matter to which the authors of the papers that follow have addressed themselves. They have done this first through the development of more general and comprehensive approaches to strengthening public administration which serve to provide the necessary framework for effective policy implementation. In addition, they have done this through the providing of some very practical case studies indicating the manner in which such policy implementation can occur.

The editors are of course grateful to many people for their assistance and support in the preparation of this volume. First of all, the staff of the Division of Public Administration and Development Management have, through their activities, provided both inspiration and guidance in terms of trying to better understand the most effective means by which the Millennium Development Goals can be implemented. Likewise, the staff of the Institute for Public Management and Community Service at Florida International University has provided great support in the actual preparation of this manuscript. In particular, Rebecca Fernandez and Viviana Quintero have devoted much attention to the preparation of this manuscript.

Of course, the co-editors are highly indebted to each of the member of the Committee of Experts who prepared the papers for this volume. We are also very indebted to the two individuals who have very effectively led the Committee of Experts on Public Administration, the Honorable Apolo R. Nsibambi, Prime Minister of Uganda and Madam Jocelyne Bourgon, the President-Emeritus of the Canada School of Public Service.

Guido Bertucci
Allan Rosenbaum

Contents

Introduction

by

Guido Bertucci

and

*Allan Rosenbaum**

Certainly, one of the boldest, indeed probably the boldest, initiative ever undertaken by any multi-national organization to improve the human social and economic condition is the set of goals found in the United Nations Millennium Declaration. In the year 2000, heads of government and state from countries throughout the world came together at the United Nations to commit themselves to the achievement of a series of profoundly far reaching and important social and economic goals. Taken together, the achievement of these goals will profoundly change for the better the nature of life for half of the planet's population. These very important, and ultimately highly liberating, goals are contained in the United Nations Millennium Declaration, and they focus upon:

- Upholding human rights, and fostering democracy and good governance;
- Ensuring peace, security and disarmament;
- Promoting development and poverty eradication;
- Fostering environmental protection;
- Protecting the vulnerable; and
- Meeting the special needs of Africa.

All too often however organizations, and nations as well, establish lofty goals but do not take the key steps needed for their implementation. In this monograph, an effort will be made to go beyond a simple description of these goals and understand and examine a key element of the means for their achievement – the capacity of governments to implement the

---

* Guido Bertucci is Director of the Division for Public Administration and Development Management, Department of Economic and Social Affairs, United Nations, New York, New York, U.S.A. and Allan Rosenbaum is Director of the Institute for Public Management and Community Service and Professor of Public Administration at Florida International University, Miami, Florida, U.S.A.

required programs and policy changes. It is here that the role of the state and its public administration, become central. Fundamental to the achievement of the Millennium Development Goals is the achievement of various very specific targets. These include the following:

GOALS	TARGETS
1. Eradicate Extreme Poverty and Hunger	1. Halve, between 1990 and 2015, the proportion of people whose income is less than a dollar a day.
	2. Halve, between 1990 and 2015, the proportion of people who suffer from hunger.
2. Achieve Universal Primary Education	3. Ensure that, by 2015, children everywhere, boys and girls alike, will be able to complete a full course of primary schooling.
3. Promote Gender Equality and Empower Women	4. Eliminate gender disparity in primary and secondary education, preferably by 2005 and at all levels of education no later than 2015.
4. Reduce Child Mortality	5. Reduce by half, between 1990 and 2015, the under – 5 mortality rate.
5. Improve Maternal Health	6. Reduce by three-quarters, between 1990 and 2015, the maternal mortality rate.
6. Combat HIV.AIDS, Malaria & Other Diseases	7. Have halted and begun to reverse the spread of HIV/AIDS by 2015.
	8. Have halted and begun to reverse the incidence of malaria and other

	major diseases by 2015.
7. Ensure Environmental Sustainability	9. Integrate the principles of sustainable development into country policies and programmes and reverse the loss of environmental resources.
	10. Halve, by 2015, the proportion of people without sustainable access to safe drinking water.
	11. Achieve a significant improvement in the lives of at least 100 million slum dwellers by 2020.
8. Develop a Global Partnership for Development	12. Further develop an open, rule-based, predictable, non-discriminatory trading and financial system (including a commitment to good governance, development and poverty reduction) both nationally and internationally.
	13. Address the special needs of the least developed countries through measures including tariff-and-quota-free access for exports, an enhanced programme of debt relief and a cancellation of official bilateral debt, and more generous official development assistance for countries committed to poverty reduction.
	14. Address special needs of land-locked countries and small islands developing states.
	15. Deal comprehensively with the

	debt problem of developing countries through national and international measures in order to make debt sustainable in the long term.
	16. In cooperation with developing countries, develop and implement strategies for decent and productive work for youth.
	17. In cooperation with pharmaceutical companies, provide access to affordable essential drugs in developing countries.
	18. In cooperation with the private sector, make available the benefits of new technologies, especially information and communication technologies.

If there is a single unifying element that underlies each of the 18 target objectives that derive from the Millennium Development Goals, it is their dependence upon effective governance and public administration for their achievement. In each and every instance, reaching the target objective will require effective and aggressive action on the part of government. This in turn obviously requires the existence of needed government capacity and that, in turn, requires effective public administration. However, the public administration required must be of a special type – a public administration that has implicit in it a commitment not just to effective management, but also to making the world a better place.

This is not a neutral public administration - which in the past has been a central objective of administration and management in the public sector. It is rather a public administration committed to building a just society not just for part of human kind but for all of human kind. It is the kind of public administration that was called for in the United Nations' first public sector report, *Globalization and the State, 2001*, where it boldly states that "eradicating poverty and ensuring sustainable development should form the raison d'etra of public administration". This involves neither a "new" public administration nor an "old" public administration. Rather it involves a strong and capable public administration dedicated to the belief that effective public programs are the result of committed and skillful public administrators and that public administration has a central role to play in making the world a better place.

Because the Millennium Development Goals are designed to bring about a fundamental restructuring of the situation of the poor in the contemporary world, if achieved, they will certainly represent one of the most outstanding accomplishments of human kind. However, one does not achieve significant social and economic restructuring of the societies of the world without major commitments of resources and energy. Such commitment cannot be carried out in a vacuum, rather it requires a facilitative environment of effective institutions, processes and procedures. Only then is it possible to create the opportunities necessary to make real change happen. Because government is the institution which establishes the rules within which all other institutions must operate within a society, "the state", of necessity, becomes a critical player in any effort to bring about the achievement of the Millennium Development Goals.

The Millennium Development Goals however, were developed and enunciated at a time during which the issue of the role of "the state", and the administrative machinery created to implement its policies, had been undergoing over two decades of challenge and critical scrutiny. Indeed, perhaps at no time in the twentieth century has the role of government and its institutions been subject to such criticism as was the case during the last two decades of the twentieth century. Concerns about the "bloated state", and the failure of government programs and policy have been central to the political dialogue of the last quarter of the twentieth century.

Similarly, and of perhaps greater significance, have been concerns about governmental corruption and "failed states". Clearly, such realities undermine efforts to encourage economic growth and poverty reduction in very profound ways. Consequently, such conditions serve to undermine the important contribution that good governance and effective public administration can make to the achievement of the Millennium Development Goals. As Aisha Ghaus-Pasha has noted "without sound governance, no country can expect to make sustained progress in human development and poverty reduction"[1]

In part, as a response to these realities and, in part, as a means to improve the quality of governance through out the world, the United Nations established in 2001 a Committee of Experts on Public Administration. The Committee, composed of 24 of the world's most distinguished experts in the field of public administration was created in order to provide a forum by which to consider the role of government and public administration in society and the means by which that role could be most fully and effectively developed. Meeting more or less annually, the Committee undertook as its charge a re-examination of the most fundamental institutions' of public sector governance as they had developed throughout the world.

The Committee also took as part of its mandate the task of looking at those ways in which public administration and institutional governance more generally, could be mobilized and harnessed to most effectively implement the Millennium Development Goals. This report, and the essays that comprise it, represent one result of that initiative. In this volume, some of the leading figures of the Committee of Experts in Public Administration of the United Nations examine many critical issues that will be a part of shaping and reshaping the contemporary state in such a manner as to position it to most effectively implement the Millennium Development Goals.

The first of these papers is written by Werner Jann, Professor at Potsdam University and a member of the Committee of Experts and a past President of the European Group on Public Administration. He begins by addressing the nature of both the state and governance very broadly and concludes by defining a specific role for effective public administration in terms of the implementation of the Millennium Development Goals. Governance, as Jann and others define it, involves not only the state and the structures of government, but indeed all of the other major institutions of the society which play a role in shaping its basic nature - including the private sector, non-governmental organizations and the like. In order to assess the appropriate role for public administration in the current state, Jann examines the four different roles which the state has played since the end of World War II. He then puts forward the notion of a new and more sophisticated role for public administration. In

---

[1] Governance for the Millennium Development Goals: Core Issues and Good Practices, United Nations, New York, 2007, p.31.

so doing, Jann proposes the re-creation of public administration in such a manner that it can much more effectively play its necessary role in the carrying out of the programmatic activity that is a pre-requisite to the achievement of the Millennium Development Goals.

In a wide ranging essay, Luiz Carlos Bresser-Pereira, a former Minister of Reform in Brazil, and one of the leading scholars of public administration in Latin America, approaches the re-definition of the state through an examination of one of its most fundamental units of analysis, the organization. Bresser-Pereira defines different types of organizations, and their basic structure of governance, and through this develops what he characterizes as the "Structural Public Governance Model". He then provides a very useful set of criteria by which to assess the role of various organizations in creating a governance system that can make the state both more capable and more efficient as it takes on the complex task of achieving the Millennium Development Goals.

As noted at the outset, a topic of special attention and concern at the Millennium Development Summit, and for the Millennium Development Goals, is the addressing the issue of Africa and its economic development. Towards that end, South Africa's Minister for Public Service and Administration, and Committee of Experts Member, Geraldine J Fraser-Moleketi reviews the deliberations of the Committee of Experts in Public Administration and examines the extent to which the Committee has in its deliberation focused upon issues of African development. However, Fraser-Moleketi goes well beyond a simple review and builds a very strong and persuasive case that central to achieving the Millennium Development Goals in Africa is the task of building a strong state with the necessary capacity to implement the needed programs and policies. Only then can one achieve the comprehensive policy and administrative reforms that are a prerequisite for the achievement of the Millennium Development Goals.

Carrying even further the discussion of the special circumstances of Africa, and its capacity to successfully achieve the Millennium Development Goals, is a task taken on by Oscar Monteiro, a past member of the Committee of Experts and Professor at Witwatersrand University, South Africa. He begins by examining the way in which Africa's colonial heritage has impacted upon the definition of the state and the complexities that that has created in terms of establishing the institutional infrastructure necessary for developing the capacity required to achieve of the Millennium Development Goals. Monteiro suggests that

7

a particular source of strength in terms of institution building can be found in the rural areas of Africa. There he finds a strong base of social capital which enables communities to interact in an effective way with central governments in order to create the kind of responsive, citizen-oriented administrative structures necessary to the achievement of the Millennium Development Goals.

Apolo R. Nsibambi, the Prime Minister of Uganda, and a past Chairperson of the Committee of Experts, provides a practical and quite specific case study of the steps necessary to achieve one of the targets that are a part of the Millennium Development Goals – universal access to primary education. To do this, he describes and analyzes the implementation of universal primary education in Uganda. In this detailed study, Nsibambi describes the efforts of the Government of Uganda to actually implementing that part of its constitution that requires the state to "provide free and compulsory basic education". He takes us through the process that led to this effort and assesses clearly, and in detail, the results of it.

In the final essay, Patricia Sto. Thomas, the Secretary for Labor and Employment for the Philippine Republic, and a former member on the Committee of Experts, turns her attention to the issue of international migration and the manner in which it serves to help less economically-developed countries enhance the life situations of their citizens. Such migration however, is characterized by many complex problems, not the least of which is the possibility of the exploitation of individuals participating in these efforts. Sto. Thomas provides a detailed description of the manner in which the Philippine Republic has gone about protecting the rights of those involved in such activities and the complex administrative action that has been a necessary prerequisite to making this possible.

Taken together, the various essays here serve to both illuminate the manner in which governments must respond if the Millennium Development Goals are to be achieved and provide specific illustrations of the way public administration can and does play a critical role in their achievement. As the initial essays make clear, absent a strong system of public administration one cannot implement the progressive policies necessary for successfully implementing the Millennium Development Goals. As the latter essays make clear, it is the way in which the public sector interacts with its citizens, to whom it must always be accountable, that either facilitates the success of a program or its failure and in so doing insures the success or failure of efforts to achieve the Millennium Development Goals.

Perhaps most importantly, the essays in this volume demonstrate the overwhelming importance of strengthening and insuring state capacity. In far too many parts of the world, the state is a very much more fragile institution than it appears. Nevertheless, it is the state that establishes the frameworks within which all other institutions of society function. Consequently, absent an effective state it is impossible for any institution of society to function at its fullest capacity. Thus, a critical precondition to the achievement of the Millennium Development Goals is the achievement of an effective state as part of a productive system of governance. The papers that follow represent a contribution by the United Nations' Committee of Experts in Public Administration to that effort.

Public Administration Under Pressure - the Search for New Forms of Public Governance

by

Werner Jann[*]

The importance of facilitating the creation of the institutional environment needed to implement the Millennium Development Goals (MDGs) has been highlighted in the United Nations Millennium Declaration (see General Assembly resolution 55/2 and A/59/282). Consequently, over the last few years, the Committee of Experts on Public Administration (CEPA) has discussed in detail how to enhance the capacity of public administration to implement the United Nations Millennium Declaration.

In this regard, the Committee dealt with, and made recommendations on, strategies for high quality staffing in the public sector, harnessing the power of information and communication technology, the alignment of financial management capacities, and the mainstreaming of poverty reduction strategies. Following up on these discussions, the Committee began consideration of strategies for revitalizing public administration and dealt specifically with the issues of enhancing human resource capacity, the role of public administration as a consumer and producer of knowledge, and especially the revitalizing and strengthening of public administration through partnership building.

The Importance of Institutions

There developed a broad consensus, that sufficient resources -- monetary, human and social -- for poverty alleviation and development cannot come from government alone. Both the private sector and civil society will have to be involved. Public Private Partnerships (PPPs), Non Governmental Organizations (NGOs), and other civil society and business actors and institutions will have to play an increasingly important role in the future, not only in mobilizing the resources to

---

[*] Chair of Political Science, Administration and Organization, Potsdam University, Germany and member of the Committee of Experts on Public Administration of the United Nations.

reduce poverty but in delivering public goods and services more efficiently and effectively. It became also widely recognized that this requires institutions and decision-making processes that are multi-stakeholder based and beyond traditional notion of government, public administration and the state.

Dealing with partnerships thus leads to the consideration of basic questions of institutional performance and design. Institutions and institutional capacities are by now nearly universally regarded as key to pursuing socio-economic development in a country. Key challenges that public administration is facing, and will continue to face, in the next decade are therefore the co-operation between public, private and civil society actors, the improvement of economic and social decision-making institutions and processes, and especially the strengthening of the integrity, transparency and accountability of institutions and institutional arrangements.

A New Role for Public Administration

All this involves a new understanding of the role of public administration and the public sector. Public administration is here understood, in line with United Nations Development Programme (UNDP) definitions, structurally as the aggregate machinery of government, i.e. policies, rules, procedures, organizational structures, personnel and so forth funded by the State budget and in charge of the management and direction of the affairs of central, regional and local governments. This entails functionally the management and implementation of the whole set of government activities dealing with the implementation of laws, regulations and decisions of the government and the management related to the provision of public goods and services[2].

Public administration and traditional government are continually being reinvented, but in a much broader sense than understood in the traditional "New Public Management" literature and discourses (Osborne/Gaebler 1992). What is needed, and what is happening around the world, is a redefinition of the role of both governments and public administration, from defining, producing and delivering services directly,

---

[2] See: United Nations Development Programme, Democratic Governance Group, Public Administration Practice Note, Bureau for Development Policy, 2003; see also: Definition of Basic Concepts and Terminologies in Governance and Public Administration, note by the Secretariat, CEPA E/C.16/2006/4.

to increasingly facilitating and regulating the delivery of public services and public goods.

The new institutional arrangements which emerge, and which point to sustaining coordination and coherence among a wide variety of actors with different purposes and objectives, including political actors and institutions, interest groups, civil society, non-governmental and transnational organizations, are by now usually referred to as "governance". Governance is a much wider concept than government, and public administration, both structurally and functionally, and thus reflects an adjustment to new arrangements for governing a society.

Governance as the New Paradigm

Governance is undoubtedly one of the most widely used catchwords of the last decade. The so-called governance problematique has become a major focus both in research and in the political discourse of the last years.[3] It is by now used in all kinds of combinations, e.g. as global governance, corporate governance, Third Sector Governance, multi level governance, and, of course, good governance, and in all kinds of connotations and by all kinds of disciplines and professions such as economics, political science, public administration, sociology and management science. In the Social Science Citation Index (SSCI), which monitors articles in important social science journals (including economics and management) world wide, the use of the term has risen by a factor of more than 30 since 1990.

In a very broad understanding, governance is about different institutional arrangements and different forms of institutional steering. It encompasses various forms of regulating social issues and solving collective problems and thus includes hierarchical decision-making by states with a monopoly over the legitimate use of force ('governance by government'), the collaboration of governments with networks of other public and private actors ('governance with government'), as well as increasing self-regulation and self-coordination by non-state actors or civil society ('governance without government').

All this is particularly true for developed states. One could argue, that we there observe a "porosity of state boundaries" with fading borders between public, private and civil society organisations and structures.

---

[3] See e.g. Kooiman 1993; Rhodes 1997; Czempiel and Rosenau 1992

The classical "Weberian State" of a hierarchically integrated, coherent public sector and political system is challenged. Modern states are domestically integrated in tight networks of public, private and societal actors, diminishing their autonomy and their ability to directly control the character and quality of public goods and services. Still, whether these changes diminish or enhance the capacity of developed states to bring about desired social and collective outcomes is an open question.

At the same time, we are not only observing new arrangements of governance with and without government, but also mounting problems of governance within government. We witness processes of accelerated horizontal differentiation and fragmentation in the core public sector of developed states (Pollitt/Talbott 2003). The total number of public sector organizations is growing remarkably; governments subdivide their traditional – sometimes large-scale – bureaucratic organizations (ministries, departments, regional or local governments) into smaller single-purpose entities. There are several variants of this kind of autonomization: *agencification* (transfer of regulatory and service-delivering tasks to semi-autonomous or even non majoritarian agencies), *corporatization* (public corporations with their own legal status) and *privatization*. The institutional foundations and conditions of modern statehood are very colourful and mixed indeed, not only governance with government, but also governance within government turns out to be more and more challenging.

Lessons from Developed Statehood

The United Nations (UN) offers a unique vantage point from which to view these developments of public administration and governance around the globe (Bertucci/Armstrong 2005). This essay will argue, that the term governance is indeed useful to indicate a new direction in the ongoing debate about the future role of public administration and public services, and the overall role of the public sector and "the state". It will look at these changes in the developed world, in order to draw lessons for developing countries.

Obviously, there are large differences between the political and administrative problems and struggles of developed and developing statehood. There is no single model and no simple best practice of governance and administration. The idea that a single, context free set of principles for organizing public administration is functionally and normatively superior, and will over time replace all others, is not supported by empirical evidence. But the lessons learned in the developed world are relevant for other countries, because they may help them to avoid certain mistakes and exaggerations. This is particularly true for the concept of public governance, because the term is characterizing a shift away from the narrow concepts of "New Public Management", which started its worldwide dominance in the 1980s, towards a more open, participative and co-operation oriented view of public administration. Thus, here we are not interested in the academic and analytical debate about the term, but want to look at how the concept is, and has been, used and developed in a broadly normative, prescriptive, even political way by practitioners both in the public and private sectors.

Basic Concepts of Public Administration and the State

The public discourse about governance is at its core about the appropriate structures, processes and roles of public administration and the public sector, and thus also about the changing boundaries between the public and the private sectors - between governments, markets, civil society and individual citizens. As with other political and social concepts -- like democracy, planning, or management -- these issues are culture bound and highly controversial, not only between different cultures and nations, but also within single nations and communities. Concepts like bureaucratic, market, participative, flexible, or deregulated government, or the minimal, lean, active, or enabling state highlight some of these controversies. If we look at public sector reform in the last decades, different reform paths or trajectories - like marketizers, modernisers, maintainers, etc. - have been identified which indicate how different nations have reacted rather differently to the world wide movement, or fashion, of public management (Pollitt/Bouckaert 2004).

But, at the same time, it seems that certain notions of the public sector and its need for reform are more dominating of the public debate in certain periods than others. One could thus talk about the "long waves" of public sector and public administration reform, which have dominated the debate since WW2 in the developed world. In order not to be too abstract, one can use a country like Germany, as an example. There we can distinguish broadly four different phases of development, each characterized by certain common themes, catchwords and concerns. Using very broad labels, we can identify the periods of the democratic, the active, the lean and the activating state:

- *Rule of law and the democratic state*: The first phase, starting after the worst problems of World War II, were overcome by the beginning of the 1950s, was not so much concerned with the efficiency or effectiveness of public administration, but mostly about its democratic control and the rule of law. Considering the German experiences during WWII and, before that, in the Nazi-dictatorship, this is not at all surprising. Public administration before and during the war had actually been quite efficient in running and supporting a dictatorship, in suppressing democracy and minorities – indeed up to the point of organizing and running concentration and death camps.

  Consequently, discussions were not so much about efficiency, but about democratic governance, about the rule of law and the democratic control and guidance of public administration and the public services. The main concern was the "democratic failure" of the old public administration, which with very few exceptions and very little resistance had followed and, in many ways, actively supported a barbarian dictatorship. Rule of law and democracy were thus the main reform concepts of this period.

- *Planning and the active state*: Only after the democratic elements were regarded as having been widely achieved, did a new concept of the public sector gain prominence. This was labeled the "active state" and starting in the mid 1960s, planning became the new catch-phrase. This was the period of the consolidation and enlargement of the modern welfare state. It was no longer democratic failure, which was seen to be the main problem, but *market failure*.

  Government, the public sector and public administration were gaining importance, were growing and were given both an increased number, and also more and more complex tasks in the running of all kinds of public services. There was great optimism about what a strong, well organized government and public sector would be able to achieve. The main debate about public sector reform therefore centered around problems of planning and implementing large public programs. One popular answer, especially advanced by economists, were technocratic planning systems like program planning and budgetary systems (PPBS).

- *Management and the lean state*: The concepts of the *active state* and the ideas of the strong, modern welfare state were, of course, never uncontested. But only towards the end of the 1970s, after several disappointments concerning large government programmes and a looming economic crisis (in the wake of the oil crises), a new concept of the public sector gained ground. Now, government and a strong public sector were no longer seen as the solution, but as the problem for all kinds of social ills. The private sector and its practices were looked upon as the main examples and inspiration for reform.

Management became the new catch phrase, and bureaucracy the new villain. No longer market failure, but *bureaucracy failure*, or even state failure were the new villains. New Public Management (NPM) turned into a new and popular, widely traded reform concept. It should be noted though, that NPM was not only attractive for conservatives and neo-liberals, who had been suspicious of the active state all along, but also for proponents of the welfare state, because it promised "a government that works better and costs less" - thus offering hope and consolidation both for critics and supporters of strong governments and public services.

- *Governance and the enabling state*: Concepts of public managerialism, like cost accounting, benchmarking, outsourcing, privatising and similar notions are still with us and are still prominent. But since the mid 1990s a new concept of public sector reform has gained ground. Now it is no longer only the public sector which is seen as the source of all or at least most of our evils, but increasingly also the shortcomings and deficiencies of societal problem solving. Thus, the focus shifts yet again from bureaucracy to *society failure,* i.e. to a much broader failure of institutional arrangements. Civil society, social capital, partnership and participation have become some of the new catch phrases, and it is here where the new, normative and prescriptive concept of public or modern governance becomes relevant.

Obviously these few remarks provide only a very simple, rough outline of a rather complicated, controversial and always contested history -- more like a caricature than a true picture. Phases and ideologies overlap and are never as clear cut as portrayed here. History does not move in neat periods. Finally, one should bear in mind, that these concepts are building upon each other. Democracy and the rule of law are not forgotten or becoming unimportant in the active welfare state, and the same holds true for efficiency, benchmarking and managerialism in the concept of public governance.

From Public Management to Public Governance

In order to understand the basic shift in the notion and understanding of public governance, it is helpful to contrast it more closely with the all but dominating concept of New Public Management. Again, it is evident that NPM is not a single, coherent concept, but a rather complex accumulation of ideas and theories, sometimes contradictory, but mostly inspired by, and transformed from, the private sector. Furthermore, its diverse instruments and notions have not been applied uniformly, quite to the contrary. But there are still common themes, which have had a unique and quite extraordinary influence on public sector reform worldwide.

The principal problems which NPM wanted to address were concerned with the supposed inefficiency of the public sector. It is the failure of the "state", of (big) government, or more precisely of classical bureaucracy, to deliver *value for money* which lies at the core of this critique. Traditional bureaucratic organization are criticized, denounced and sometimes caricatured as ruled by *red tape* and as *organized irresponsibility*. Instead of classical Weberian values, like due process, reliability, equity and fairness, new values, like service mindedness, timeliness, customer and quality orientation are stressed. Again, this does not imply that old values become obsolete, but there are, in this view, other more important values which deserve much more attention. The public sector, so the overriding assumption, should be looked upon as a business organization, public administration as a firm, and government as a service.

But gradually in the 1990s these conceptions lost their apparent monopoly or at least their dominance. Concepts like civil society, social capital and the *enabling state* entered the scene. It was no longer just the efficiency of the public sector which was seen as the main problem, but its effectiveness. Not only was bureaucracy seen as the main obstacle to effective social problem solving but, more and more, the organizational features of society were seen as a problem. Last, but not least, civil society, so the new view held, had to take on a new role, to be strengthened and enabled to participate, to work closely with public and private actors in the tackling of collective problems. New crucial values were therefore social, political and administrative co-operation, cohesion and interdependence, public participation and civic engagement. Not only the state and public administration needed to change, but new forms

17

of interactions between state and society had to be invented, enabling new modes of societal self-regulation. 'State failure' was no longer seen as the only dilemma of public governance, but rather 'community failure'. In order to cope with these problems, more advanced patterns of negotiated public-private coordination both with market and civil society actors were needed.

While the NPM view focused very much on the public organization, its internal control and steering mechanisms and (lack of) incentives, the new governance approach shifted its attention towards the co-ordination and co-operation of public and private actors, towards network management and the combination of different modes of steering and control beyond markets and hierarchies. It was the interdependence of different public and private actors and the coherence of collective action, which gradually became the main concern. While the preferred solutions of NPM derived from experiences in the private sector and stressed decentralization, contract management, modern instruments of financial and human resources management, the new governance approach concentrated on a new division of labour between state, market and civil society. Solutions were seen, if at all possible, in the creating and strengthening of autonomous, self-regulated networks which are able to generate 'public value' even without the state.

A new concept of modern statehood became prominent, the enabling, guaranteeing or ensuring state. The task of this modern state is to guarantee the extent and the quality of public services, but not necessarily to engage in their production. Instead, it should supervise, create and encourage alternatives concerning the financing and the delivery of these services, using the whole spectrum between state, third sector, civil society and market.

From Economic to Social Institutions

Underlying these changes of basic assumptions and preferred solutions were also different theoretical premises. While NPM was inspired by models of new institutional economics (property rights, principal agents, transaction costs) and by modern management textbooks (even though these different sources sometimes contradict each others), the public governance discourse stressed again the importance of social sciences and even philosophy. Inspirations were therefore obtained from communitarianism and neo-institutional theory, which stress not only formal and informal rules as the basis for institutions, but also mental maps, both cognitive and normative assumptions and values, as important and indisputable sources of institutional arrangements.

To put the difference rather starkly, one could argue that NPM was basically concerned with the problem of 'getting incentives right', and these incentives were mainly seen as monetary incentives. If it proved impossible to establish real markets, than at least market surrogates, like benchmarks, contracts and sanctions were sought. Contrasted with that, the new emerging governance discourse was more concerned with *appropriate behaviour* -- both within the public sector and between the public and private sectors. The main problem here is 'getting institutions right'. i.e. how to ensure that not only public organisations and services, but also private ones, work together to solve social problems. Obviously public services and monetary incentives are important, but not sufficient. And institutions are not only about formal rules and incentives, but also about informal norms and 'appropriate' behavior.

Corruption is an example. One way to prevent corruption is to make it economically unattractive, either by paying public servants so much that they are no longer tempted, or by ruthlessly increasing control mechanisms. But obviously these two mechanisms will never suffice, both direct and control costs are too high. So the issue becomes how can we assure that civil servants fulfil their duties, in ways that are efficient, effective, impartial and fair? How can we create working institutions and institutional and procedural arrangements, which do not only consist of workable formal and informal rules and incentives, but also take account of appropriate cognitive and normative values?

Normative Foundations of Public Governance

The governance perspective can be interpreted as a reaction against the NPM-movement which, at least for some observers and participants, turned out to be too narrow, focusing too much on the internal mechanisms, control instruments and incentives of single organisations and neglecting the complex interactions of different organizational and institutional arrangements and value foundations within the public sector and beyond. But in a wider, somewhat more theoretical perspective, public governance is not only seen as an extension and perhaps counter-concept to NPM, but as an alternative to traditional government perceptions: governance instead of government.

In this view, public governance is not only about new institutional arrangements, but also about new, or at least modified, public values. The traditional values of economic welfare, political freedom, social justice and solidarity -- which characterize both the foundation and images of the active and the lean state -- are still valid. But they are interpreted somewhat differently. Economic welfare is specified as economic vitality, which has to be achieved in order to guarantee general and social welfare. Political freedom entails more participation and civic engagement, and social justice is seen as the equality of chances, not of outcomes. Solidarity finally is defined as social inclusion and cohesion.

But concepts of public governance go beyond the re-definition or "re-invention" of traditional values. They also contain new images of the appropriate roles and functions of citizens, societies and states. In all concepts of traditional government, be they bureaucratic or managerial, citizens are looked upon as either voters, consumers, clients or customers of public services. The controversy whether citizens are or at least should be treated as customers has been a standard favourite of proponents and opponents of NPM. Public governance concepts acknowledge that citizens perform all these kinds of roles. But their main argument is that citizens should be looked upon and treated foremost as activist and co-producers of social services and values. They are neither merely voters, nor dependent customers or clients, but are first of all partners of social co-operation and negotiation. *Empowerment* of citizens is therefore one of the new preoccupations.

This image is also extended towards society. It is thus no longer just perceived as the - more or less active - beneficiary of state intervention and public programmes. Similarly, state-society interactions are no longer only characterized by pluralist bargaining or corporatist interest mediation, or even clientelistic dependence. Instead society, its citizens and organisations are seen as indispensable active partners in solving collective problems and creating public values. The ideal picture is that of an active civil society, and the preferred solution is societal self regulation - if at all possible, without state or public interference.

This, in the end, leads to another perception of the state. Conventional government concepts tend to have a rather state-centred view of the world. Traditionally, the state is sovereign, both internally and externally, and is also the only, or at least the predominant, source of all kinds of legitimate institutional arrangements. Concerning their own organization, traditional states therefore are hierarchically integrated, with long and complicated horizontal and vertical chains of production. Again, the public governance concept sketches a different image. The modern state is no longer the all inclusive sovereign system, but just one social system amongst others. The appropriate picture of modern statehood is thus not the hierarchical integration, but the management of plural networks.

Democratic governance is consequently no longer merely defined by parties, interest groups, parliaments and a quasi state monopoly in the ensuing conflict resolution and welfare state arrangements. Instead, the articulation and co-ordination of collective interests is characterized by direct participation and a wide variety of negotiated patterns of public-private co-ordination and co-operation. Several diverse welfare arrangement are possible and desirable, and some of them with very little, or without, state interference.

The Importance of Public Administration

What does all this mean for conventional public administration? Concepts of public governance do not assume that traditional public organisations or public services will or should disappear, or that all kinds of public tasks will be taken over by the market or the private sector. But it is assumed that, in changing surroundings and institutional arrangements, public organisations, structures and processes will have to adjust.

Public organisations and public employees will continue to play an important role in policy formation and implementation, and perhaps an even stronger one in performance measurement and policy evaluation. But these roles do not imply any kind of monopoly. Policy formation will be ever more about the negotiation of new and improved policy arrangements. There will be no longer - if there ever has been - a one and only, unitary view of the public good and public welfare. Public administration does not have a monopoly, neither of the values nor of the contents, structures and procedures of public policies. Conflict resolution and consensus building are therefore at least as important as information and analysis.

Concerning the implementation of public policies and the production of public services, the task will neither be to defend the existing division of labour and the erstwhile boundaries of the public sector; nor to dismantle or privatize at all costs. The *enabling* or *ensuring state* depends on the steering capacities of its public organisations. But the management and steering of public goods and services does not imply that they have to be produced within the public sector. Out-sourcing and contracting-out are common in modern governance arrangements, but the task of public administration is not limited towards the separation and negotiation of formerly unified tasks and costs. Instead, the initiation and organization of new arrangements for the co-production of services, involving public, private and third-sector organizations as well as civil society and individual actors is called for. Neither the protection, nor the simple transfer of responsibilities and performance is called for, but shared responsibilities and the activation of performance and self help is required. Public governance is about shared obligations, not reduced or abandoned ones.

- the state remains a "State of Law", its public employees however, are not just bureaucrats and experts in law and procedure, but belong also to the managerial profession with a focus on performance and customers;
- citizens have rights and duties, but the customer role becomes part of the citizen role;
- there remains a distinct public service with its own features (status, culture, and conditions), but its traditional neutrality and concern with legality is amended with commitments to policy objectives and concerns with results -- which create a professional culture of quality and service;
- the ex-ante concern with process and procedure to guarantee the legality, and legitimacy of decisions is amended with an ex-post concern with results which becomes also part of the procedure to guarantee economy, efficiency and effectiveness;
- legitimacy is therefore not just based on legality, but also on the economy, efficiency and effectiveness of the functioning of the state and its policies.

The Structural Public Governance Model and the Implementation of the Millennium Development Goals

by
*Luiz Carlos Bresser-Pereira**

The successful implementation of the United Nations Millennium Development Goals would represent a major achievement for the entirety of humankind. While the implementing of many strategies will be required for the achievement of this critically important agenda, none is more important than the sustained economic development of the countries for which the achievements of the Goals represent the greatest challenge. This of course raises the issue of what factors are necessary to contribute to sustained economic developments.

Increasingly, the critical importance of the effective state is recognized as being central to successful economic development. While private entrepreneurs will provide most of the investment necessary for economic development, a capable state will be crucial in creating the institutional and economic conditions for capital accumulation and growth. Today, it is common knowledge that effective institutions are central to promoting economic development. The state itself is the central institution in modern societies; it is an organization that itself gives rise to normative institutions. Besides being capable of democratically constructing an adequate legal framework for the achievement of society's goals, the state, or public administration, must be effective and efficient in providing the services that citizens demand of it. If these assumptions are accepted, some questions arise concerning the organization and management of the state. In this paper, we shall examine the question of "what kind of organization or public administration makes for a capable state?" Just a professional civil service? Or are contemporary ideas related to broader public management reform – specifically, to what will be called the 'structural public governance model' – also part of the package even for developing countries?

* Professor at the Getulio Vargas Foundation, Brazil and a member of the Committee of Experts on Public Administration of the United Nations. He thanks Evelyn Levy, Humberto Martins and Michael James for their comments.

For this kind of question there are no simple or definite answers, but, since they are loaded with ideology, a candid discussion of them may clarify the issues. If what is needed is just a Weberian type of bureaucracy, consisting of well-selected and well-trained professionals acting without discretion in law enforcement, and a hierarchical and centralized organization with defined lines of authority, there is no need for this discussion. But if, besides a professional civil service, modern states require senior civil servants to have more discretion and to be more accountable for their decisions, and the organization of the state to be more decentralized and involve all sort of partnerships, we have a problem that is worthy of analysis.

Center-left academics tend to believe that public management reform is intrinsically neo-liberal and hostile to the social state, probably because this type of reform began in the United Kingdom in the mid-1980s when a conservative government was in power, and also because some of its first proponents were conservative in political terms. Is this true? Or is public management, on the contrary, a neutral instrument which can be used by a conservative administration that wants to dismantle the social state but also by a progressive administration that is concerned with a more equal distribution of income in society? Again, since this reform was originally adopted by developed countries, is it inapplicable to developing countries? Should they faithfully observe the sequencing rule – first complete civil service reform and only then tackle public management reform? It will be argued here that the sequencing rule is misguided, and that there is no reason why civil service reform should not be combined with public management reform. This, for instance, is the experience of Brazil, a country that since 1995 has been involved in progressive public management reform at federal, state and municipal levels.[4] But we will not discuss specific reforms here. Rather, a specific model of public management reform – the structural public governance model – will be presented and, on this basis, its possible progressive or conservative character, and its appropriateness to developing countries, will be examined.

This model of public management reform is characterized as the 'structural public governance model' in that it includes structural reform of the state organization, in addition to major changes in the process of managing personnel and achieving objectives. Public management

---

[4] The reform in Brazil began when the new Ministry of Federal Administration and Reform of the State (MARE) was approved by the Presidential Committee of the Reform of the State. See the *White Paper on the Reform of the State Apparatus* (MARE, 1995).

reform is the second major administrative reform experienced by the modern capitalist state. In its first version, the modern state was absolutist, and adopted a patrimonial administration. In the second part of the nineteenth century, the more advanced capitalist countries undertook the first major administrative reform – civil service or bureaucratic reform.[5] This represented immense progress. Yet, after World War II, the countries that were using the state as an instrument to promote economic development realized that public administration needed to be more flexible. As a consequence, state investments were channeled to state-owned enterprises, and some agencies were created that enjoyed various degrees of autonomy. These were attempts to make the state organization more flexible and, for that reason, more effective in promoting economic development. Yet it was only in the 1980s that it became clear that such developmental attempts would only make sense if they were accompanied by a new form of managing the state organization: a new public management. With this realization, a second major reform of the state apparatus was beginning. The first countries to recognize this need and embark on public management reform were the United Kingdom, Australia and New Zealand.

There are many accounts of the new public management that emerged from the reforms in these three countries, which were soon followed by others, including Brazil. The modern literature on "new public management", or just public management, is substantial. Here, the structural public governance model will be defined based on the Brazilian experience of public management reform since 1995, when a social democratic administration took office, and on the British experience, which served as the principal reference for Brazil's efforts. The structural public governance model is an historical model because it uses an historical method, drawing from the experience of countries that undertook the reform, and seeks to generalize from its main characteristics. Yet it is also a normative model because it is impossible not to be normative on questions that involve political theory and public policy – specifically the reform of the state organization.[6] It is a model of public management reform which should be considered by other developing countries as a tool for their economic growth. It is a structural model because, as we will see, it is not limited to management strategies but involves more than organizational changes: it implies changes in the state structure, because all kinds of public-private partnerships are involved and because the social and scientific services that society

---

[5] On that reform, besides Max Weber's classical works, see particularly Silberman (1993).
[6] For the Brazilian reform, see Bresser-Pereira and Spink, eds. (1998), and Bresser-Pereira (2004). For the reform in the OECD countries, see Pollitt and Bouckaert (2000).

requires the state to provide are contracted out to non-state organizations. It is a governance model because it involves other actors in the governing process besides the government itself.

The Organizational Aspect of the Structural Public Governance Model

The structural public governance model includes an organizational aspect and a management or accountability aspect. On the one hand, there is the problem of how to structure or organize state services -- what the strategic core of the state should do, what to delegate to agencies, and which services to contract out; on the other hand, is the question of how to manage the whole system – a matter of process rather than of structure.

The organizational aspect of the structural public governance model deals not with the role of the state but with its structure. In the nineteenth century, Marx said that the state was the 'executive committee of the bourgeoisie'. At that time, he might well have been right, but in contemporary democracies the state is, rather, society's main instrument of collective action: it is the basic tool that national societies use to achieve their political goals. Business elites continue to have a major influence, but the middle class and even the poor have a say. Together, and despite the conflict between them, they constitute the nation, and the more developed a country or nation-state is, the more able the nation is to use the state as an instrument to achieve its political objectives (social order, liberty, well-being, justice, and protection of the environment) in a competitive global economy.

In modern democracies, the role of the state is ultimately decided by the voters and the politicians they elect. They will decide whether the state should secure social rights in terms of education, health care, culture, and social security, as well as how the government will support national economic development. Yet they probably will not get involved directly in the more technical discussion of how the state should be organized. Once having decided politically on the role of the state, citizens will need to give the state an efficient structure consistent with that role. The structural public governance model presented here aims to achieve this requirement, with the advantage that it is relatively neutral in ideological terms: it will work for a social democratic state, but also for a neo-liberal one. Yet, to be efficient and general, the model does not limit itself to the state apparatus. Its structural character requires a larger horizon, encompassing the different critical activities that are performed by the state and by other social actors in a modern nation-state, and the basic types of ownership and corresponding organizations that characterize modern societies

First, we have four distinct types of ownership and corresponding organization: (a) state ownership, (b) public, non-state ownership, (c) corporatist ownership, and (d) private ownership. The distinction between public and private is not based on the type of law to which the organization is subject (public or private law), but on the organization's objectives: if the objective is profit, it is private; if it is the public interest, it is public; if it is the defense of group interests, it is corporatist. In order to distinguish state from public, non-state organizations, a second criterion – in this case a legal one – is required. If the employees of a public organization are subject to civil or private law, the organization is public, non-state – it is public because it is not-for-profit and oriented to the public interest, but not part of the state organization; if it is subject to public or administrative law, if its employees are 'statutory civil servants', we have a state organization – and such an organization is part of the state apparatus. According to this second criterion, universities like the University of California, despite being called 'state universities', are not state, but public, non-state organizations, because their employees are not public servants whose salaries are decided at government level and guaranteed by the state.

Among public, non-state organizations, it is necessary to distinguish service organizations - which provide principally education, health care and social assistance - from political advocacy or social accountability organizations, although some of them, such as Oxfam, perform both roles. The distinction between public, non-state and corporatist organizations is important because the former are supposedly concerned with the public interest,[7] while the latter - of which trade unions and professional associations are the best examples - explicitly defend group interests which may or may not coincide with the public interest. Among public, non-state organizations, the social accountability or political advocacy organizations (also called *stricto senso* 'non-governmental organizations' - NGOs), together with corporatist ones, form the modernly called 'organizations of civil society'. If we add to them the public, non-state service organizations, the sum of these non-

---

[7] Many 'supposedly' public non-state organizations are, in fact, private since they effectively sponsor private interests. This is just one distortion among the many in all social systems.

profit organizations form the 'third sector' (also called the 'associative sector' or the 'social sector').

Second, the organizational aspect of the structural public governance model distinguishes several basic forms of activity involving production and the exercise of power which are carried out in a modern society: (1) the specific activities of the state involving the exercise of state power and the management of state resources or of tax revenues, which require a further distinction between (1.1) the core activities of policy formulation and (1.2) the implementation of policies requiring the use of state power; (2) the activities of social advocacy or social accountability; (3) the provision of social and scientific services which society decides that the state is responsible for, such as health care, education, scientific research, and cultural promotion; (4) the defense or promotion of corporatist interests; and (5) the production of goods and services for competitive markets.

These distinctions of ownership and organization are graphically presented in Table 1.

Table 1: Activities, Forms of Ownership, and Organizations

Given these two basic classifications – of forms of ownership and of activities – the model suggests the types of organizations which are supposed to perform the different activities. The exclusive activities

	State ownership	Public non-state ownership	Corporatist ownership	Private ownership
Exclusive activities: policy formulation	Secretaries or Departments	X	X	X
Exclusive activities: implementation	Agencies	X	X	X
Social accountability activities	X	Public advocacy organizations	X	
Defense of corporative interests	X	X	Unions & associations	X
Supply of social and scientific services	X	Social organizations	X	Charities
Production of market goods and services	X	X	X	Business enterprises

of the state, involving the use of state power and policy formulation, will be performed by secretariats or departments at the strategic core of the government where politicians and senior civil servants work together. The implementation of policies still involving state power will be the responsibility of administratively autonomous executive and regulatory agencies. The latter will also have some political autonomy in so far as they are supposed to regulate prices and quality in oligopolist industries as if the respective market was competitive: in principle, they are not supposed to define other policies, which will remain the prerogative of elected officials. Social and scientific services supported by the state - like hospitals, museums, universities, and research centers - will be delivered by public, non-state organizations. If they are contracted out by government, they are (or should be called) 'social organizations';[8] if they are principally financed by the private sector, 'charities' is probably the best word to characterize such service organizations. Finally, producers of goods and services for the market are supposed to be privatized - except when they are natural monopolies, as in the case of urban water supply.

Table 1 summarizes the organizational aspect of the model. It implies a set of decisions: some are self-explanatory, other involve major debate. For instance, why contract out social and scientific services to non-profit service organizations rather than letting them be delivered directly by the state? Because they are non-exclusive activities of the state (activities that the other three sectors can also execute), and may be more efficiently performed by autonomous social organizations under contract and duly made accountable to society and to the government. Why not contract them out to private enterprise? Because the information asymmetries that pervade the markets for such services are huge, and because major human rights issues are involved. In any case, while in sectors such as university education or hospitals, the advantages of contracting out to social organizations are clear and reform should be expedited; in other sectors, such as basic education, change will have to be gradual. While we have an example of the extremely successful use of public non-state organizations in the US university system, no country supplies a similar example in the area of basic education. There is no doubt that reform will work in the direction of more flexible public, non-state systems, but such reform will need to be piecemeal.

---

[8] The expression 'social organization' was used in the Brazilian Public Management Reform of 1995–98 in a federal and several state and municipal laws.

Thus, the structural public governance model involves state; public, non-state; corporatist; and private organizations. Since these organizations are increasingly interdependent, forming all kinds of networks, public management models are often identified with public-private-third sector partnerships. The expression is not wholly adequate because it plays down the state, as if it was not endowed with the powers which led Max Weber to define it as 'the monopoly of legitimate power'. Yet the concepts of partnership and network are useful to underline that the state is not supposed to perform directly all the roles or responsibilities that voters and the law attribute to it. As governments have been able to contract out construction and other auxiliary services to business firms, they can contract out the delivery of social and scientific services to public, non-state organizations without renouncing their responsibilities.

This contracting out or outsourcing has interesting consequences in terms of the size of the state apparatus. If one defines the size of the state by the number of people directly hired, the state will be small: the state will just hire high-level senior civil servants, recruited among the best young talent at society's disposal, well trained, well paid, and from whom will be required not only an appropriate republican ethos but high standards of competence. Yet, if the size of the state is defined by the tax burden or total state expenditures in relation to gross domestic product (GDP), it may remain large if society decides to continue having a social welfare state. In that case, the state organization contracted out service delivery only, and retained responsibility for their finance and performance.

What is the logic behind such division of roles between the state and society in the supply of basic social and scientific services, with the state financing and controlling the services, and public non-state service organizations providing them? The state has such a strategic role in society that it should retain only those activities which are specific or exclusive to it – activities which involve state power, such as policy-making, defining the major institutions organizing the whole society, and guaranteeing security for its members. These roles are monopolistic and need, on the one hand, to be performed by high-level personnel and, on the other hand, to be fully accountable to society. While the services themselves must be offered efficiently, these are strategic roles performed directly by government and must be effective and of high quality. These roles relate to ideas and decisions, not products and services, which is why they require some of the best talents of each society. This is also why, despite the use of high-level personnel, the actions taken within the state organization require a costly system of accountability.

Although the social and scientific services are not exclusive to the state, society may (and should) finance crucial social and scientific services that society decides to make freely, or quasi-freely, available to all. The act of financing the service organizations and of making them accountable to the state is also an exclusive activity of the state, in so far as the civil servants performing this role are using tax revenue resources. In contrast, implementing the policies and supplying social and scientific services financed by the state, does not need the direct involvement of statutory civil servants. Although also complex, these are substantially simpler activities. Their outcomes may be more objectively quantified and compared. In certain cases, the activities may be subject to an accounting process based on administered competition for excellence. Both facts reduce the control costs involved. On the other hand, these service activities require a flexibility that the state organization does not have, whatever the management practices it adopts. Thus, they may be more efficiently delivered by public non-state service organizations.

The Management Aspect and the New Forms of Accountability

Besides the organizational aspect, the structural public governance model has a specific management aspect. The objective is to make the administration more flexible and the managers more motivated. Most of the ideas originated in management practices developed during the twentieth century by private organizations. The management aspect emphasizes 'client-citizen' oriented action, and two of its three specific accountability mechanisms – administration by objectives and administrative competition for excellence – were borrowed from business administration. This should not be misunderstood. The principles that orient public management continue to flow from political theory and political science rather than business management. The objective is the public interest, not profits; the coordination system is administrative and legal, rather than performed by the market. And the third specific accountability mechanism – social accountability performed by political advocacy organizations – is exclusive to the public realm. Following Ranson and Stewart's (1994) concerns, we are speaking of a 'management for the public domain', not for the private one. When one speaks of citizen-client orientation in this context, there is no reduction of the citizen to a consumer, but a fuller recognition of the citizen's rights.

To express in a nutshell the managerial character of the model, one could say that public management reform seeks to make civil servants more autonomous and more accountable: more autonomous from strict regulations and direct supervision, and more accountable to the strategic core of the state and to society. Another way of putting it would be that public management reform is a process of decentralization – of delegation of authority to lower levels, while making the strategic core of the state stronger and social accountability mechanisms more effective. Yet the decentralization does not go all the way: a central characteristic of public management reform is to separate policy formulation, which remains centralized, from execution, which is decentralized. Still another way of explaining public management reform is to think not in terms of government -- but of governance. The English term 'government' is often confused with 'state', but even in other languages, where such confusion does not arise, it is useful to distinguish 'government' from 'governance'. Government, as an entity, is formed by the top decision-making bodies of the state; as a communications flow, it is the decision-making process of public officials (politicians and senior public servants). Governance involves also a process, but a larger one, as it conveys the idea that public non-state organizations or organizations of civil society, business firms, individual citizens, and international organizations also participate in the decision-making process, although the government remains the central actor.

Since public management reform represents a further step in relation to civil service reform, it adopts a new form of control or accountability. The three classical bureaucratic forms of accountability are exhaustive regulations, direct hierarchical supervision, and auditing mechanisms. The three typical managerial forms are management by outcomes or objectives, administrative competition for excellence, and social accountability. The three new forms do not overturn the classical ones but do partially replace them. Management by results is a form of decentralization: the supervisory secretary defines the objectives and the performance indicators with the participation of the agency or of its manager, who is assured the administrative autonomy – personal and financial – to achieve them. Administrative competition for excellence does not mean market coordination of public services but compares the standards or benchmarks achieved by different public organizations that deliver the same service in different regions. The difference in relation to management by objectives is that the standards or performance indicators emerge from the effective accomplishments of the different agencies or services rather than from a management contract - which would have to define such performance indicators somewhat arbitrarily, and based only on previous experience. Social accountability means the use of civil society organizations, including councils of citizens, to keep public services and public officers under control.

Under public management reform, decentralization is achieved by the transfer of service provision to agencies and social organizations. Policy formulation remains centralized, but the central authority is able to delegate powers in so far as it is able to use managerial accountability mechanisms effectively. While bureaucratic control mechanisms imply a centralized organization, managerial accountability mechanisms are consistent with decentralization – a decentralization that does not mean reducing, but rather increasing, managerial control over outcomes. This is true because this type of managerial decentralization is just a provisional delegation of authority: the central manager retains the option of reversing it whenever it is not working. It is quite different from the political decentralization involved in transferring fiscal resources from the central state to the provinces or local municipalities. Such an option may also be good for large nation states, but is not easily reversed. Often it is the outcome of a political demand rather than of a government strategy. For that reason, the issue of the federal versus the unitary state should not be confused with public management reform.

Public management involves strategic planning. While in bureaucratic administration, planning is limited to the law and regulation, without individual cases or possible responses from adversaries being taken into account, managerial planning involves a detailed definition of the processes to be followed and of the strategies to be adopted, depending on the responses. Thus, public management reform does not imply less managerial work but often more, despite involving decentralization. This is so true that one distortion that may easily arise is that of excess and costly planning. But, if this mistake is avoided, the efficiency gains from public management reform will be substantial.

Public management reform extensively uses information technology, which is able to deliver enormous labor savings besides allowing for large economies in the state's purchasing activity. Yet one should not identify public management reform with the use of information technology. Independently of the type of administration –

managerial or bureaucratic – such a major innovation would be used by the state. In the case of managerial accountability mechanisms, well-used information technology makes further decentralization viable.

Only within a democratic framework is it possible to accept the high degree of autonomy assigned to managers in public management reforms. While bureaucratic public administration was created within a liberal but not democratic state, and was concerned with strict controls, public management reform is unthinkable without democracy. The autonomy that the public manager assumes, the possibility of making decisions instead of just executing the law, is checked *a posteriori* by managerial accountability mechanisms, particularly by the social accountability mechanism involving pressure for more transparency and an increased investigative role on the part of the media. Given that public management reform presupposes democracy, and that the values related to the autonomy of civil servants are well integrated in society, their formal tenure or stability can be made more flexible, more similar to that which exists in the labor market.[9] Their pay may and should be more flexible, reflecting their performance. It should also be higher because the salaries of public managers would be competitive with salaries of the private sector in so far as the private and the public labor market cease to be separated (while the wages of non-skilled public servants would tend to equalize with the correspondent jobs in the private sector).[10] They will be made accountable through public management accountability mechanisms rather than through bureaucratic ones. Finally, in the managerial system, the republican civil service ethos, so important for this type of job, will be better assured than in the bureaucratic one, because public managers will be few in number, well-paid and highly prestigious.

This possibility is challenged by many, particularly by adherents of public choice theory, which, transferring to the public sphere the economists' view of the behavior of businessmen competing in the market, see civil servants as ignoring the public interest. They would just make trade-offs between rent-seeking and occupation of higher positions in the bureaucratic hierarchy (which could be endangered by the rent-

---

[9] In Brazil there was no flexibilization of entrance examinations because the country had not achieved the reasonable degree of equalization of the public and private labor markets which is required for such flexiblilization to work well..

[10] In bureaucratic administrations, like the French or the Brazilian one, salaries of public managers tend to be smaller than salaries of private ones, while wages of low level public servants tend to be higher than their counterpart in the private sector. With public management reform, this difference gradually disappears.

seeking), as politicians would just make trade-offs between rent-seeking and the desire to be reelected. This is a smart assumption when one wants to give mathematical precision to the political sciences: political actors' behavior would be as predictable as economic agents' behavior in the market. Yet such a simplifying assumption grossly misconceives political and bureaucratic behavior, which, unlike economic behavior, is motivated not only by private interests but also by the public interest.[11] Given the different expectations involving the behavior of businessmen on the one hand and of politicians and civil servants on the other, the social legitimacy involved will differ as between the two areas. While the businessman may legitimately be guided by private interests, the public official cannot, because society does not accept such an approach. Thus, given the demands of society, it is reasonable to expect from a small group of prestigious civil servants, chosen from among the brightest young people of each society that they will be able to establish and conform to high standards of republican behavior.

As was asked in relation to the type of structure, we now ask in relation to this form of administration: what is the underlying logic? Why give public officials more autonomy and make them more accountable? First and foremost, because we are speaking of public managers with entrepreneurial qualities whose motivation depends on their autonomy. Motivation in the state, as well in private organizations, does not depend only on economic incentives, or on the republican ethos: it depends also on the satisfaction of a basic need of entrepreneurial personalities, a need to achieve. Competent managers are achievement-motivated. They want power to do things, and they need autonomy to do them. Second, because more autonomy means the possibility of adapting actions to complex and changing conditions – conditions that strict regulations cannot predict. If the risks involved in such higher autonomy are minimized by new forms of accountability, its efficiency advantages are obvious.

Importing Institutions for Economic Development

The structural public governance model, like all ideal types, is not fully present in reality, but in one way or another it is being developed by most rich countries - except Germany, France, Spain and Japan. Some questions follow. Does the model reduce the influence of civil servants who, in the patrimonial administration of the absolutist state, share power with the dominant aristocratic class, and, in the bureaucratic administration of the liberal state, were allied to the

---

[11] This does not mean that the assumption of full rationality is acceptable for economic behavior: it just means that in this area, depending on the level of abstraction, it may make sense.

entrepreneurial class, and played a major role in formulating and implementing national strategies of growth? If the answer to these questions is negative, would this model of state reform have, as a trade-off, the effect of concentrating income or increasing inequality? And, if this question also receives a negative answer, is the model applicable to developing countries?

The first question is central, because reforming the state organization makes sense only if it contributes to enhancing state capacity – and, if it does, it will increase the prestige and influence of the public officials, both politicians and senior civil servants, who manage it. The assumption behind this claim is that, historically, economic development was possible only after the first industrialized countries realized their 'national revolution', that is, the building of capable states. The state, as the nation's instrument of collective action, is a prerequisite for economic growth, initially because it offers secure internal markets to entrepreneurs, and generally because the existence of a state (organization and institutions) enables a nation to achieve its main political goals, particularly economic development. A nation is essentially a society or a group of people sharing a common destiny and using the state as their key instrument of collective action. Historical experience shows that only a nation-state formed out of a strong or cohesive nation and a capable state administration is able to devise and follow a national strategy of economic growth.

Public management reform, understood in terms of the structural public governance model, is essentially aimed at increasing the state's capacity to guarantee social and republican rights without incurring the inefficiencies that characterized the twentieth- century bureaucratic welfare state. The idea is not to replace the social state by an 'enabling state', as neo-liberal thinking proposes; it is not to consider the social state 'paternalistic' in so far as it establishes safety nets, and to replace it by a form of state that 'empowers individuals to compete in the market'. People must indeed be prepared to compete, but they also need protection, require security – particularly the weaker and the less able. It is true that, in some cases, policies adopted in the name of public management reform weakened the state instead of making it stronger. This was the case in New Zealand in the 1990s, during a few years of conservative administration after the Labour Party started the reform. But the conservatives lost the subsequent election, and the reform was resumed on reasonable terms. The central economic idea of reforming the state is to make better use of tax revenues – to provide better services at lower cost – or, in other words, to make the state organization more efficient in the use of money that is always relatively scarce.

The reform does not discuss how the government can be more legitimate – this is a question of political or democratic reform – but it indirectly contributes to the legitimacy of the political system as a whole. It is interested in knowing how governments, how elected and non-elected public officials at the strategic core of the state take the decisions that improve governance, but its specific realm is the organization and management of the state. On the one hand, it proposes a criterion for the division of labor among state, public-non state, corporatist, and private organizations; on the other hand, it suggests policies to make public managers more motivated and more efficient by making them autonomous and accountable. In the competitive capitalist world in which we live, efficiency is required everywhere. Thus, there is a saying – 'do not throw good money after bad' – which is often used to reject paying taxes and financing needed social services. A state organization which undergoes public management reform becomes more efficient and, for that reason, more capable and more legitimate.

With public management reform, senior public servants working principally in the strategic core of the state become also more respected. Since they are used to classical bureaucratic principles, civil servants usually start by distrusting new ideas. Yet reform will be successful only if it can count on their support and initiative. In fact, most public management reform in the last 20 years was effective when senior civil servants realized that such reform represented an important opportunity for competent civil servants – when they understood that the old bureaucratic practices were weakening the state and demoralizing the civil service, and decided to engage in reform. In modern capitalist societies, a state organization is legitimate, and its personnel respected, when it is an effective instrument for economic growth. It was the practical confirmation of this that made it possible for the original public management reforms in the United Kingdom, Australia and New Zealand in the 1980s to spread to most developed countries in the following decade.[12]

Once it is accepted that public management reform strengthens the state, increases the legitimacy of the democratic regime, and promotes economic growth, the next question is whether this is achieved

---

[12] The survey by Pollitt and Bouchaert (2000), found in the 2004 edition of their book, is definitive on this subject.

at the cost of more social inequality. Given that the reform often reduces the number of non-managerial jobs in the state bureaucracy, and assumed that these low level jobs tend to be better-paid than the correspondent jobs in the private sector, some concentration will occur. On the other hand, as it allows the state to devote more resources to increasing social services, it works in favor of redistribution. It is important to notice that, since the 1970s, we have lived in a time of income and wealth concentration – of rising inequality in all capitalist countries. This has been mainly a consequence of the information technology revolution, which increased the demand for skilled labor while reducing the demand for non-specialized work, and of the neo-liberal ideological wave, which after the 1970s pushed for a reduction of the welfare state, or the indirect wage. Public management reform was viewed by many as an element of this process, but the fact is that it increased the capacity of the state to provide efficiently social services which, being basically universal, contribute to social equality. In fact, public management reform is neutral in distributive terms. It may be used either to reduce or to increase direct and indirect wages. Yet, in so far as it increases state capacity, it also legitimizes increases in the state's social expenditures, and so makes it more probable that a country that adopts it will be better able to assure social rights.

Our third and last question: wouldn't public management reform be too ambitious for developing countries? Shouldn't they follow the sequencing process that is so dear to international organizations such as the World Bank?[13] Should they not first complete civil service reform, and only then get into public management reform? The response that immediately comes to mind is to agree provided that one also agrees that the country should first complete the nineteenth century mechanical revolution, and only after that engage in the information technology revolution... If this answer is too impatient, another way of putting the problem is to argue that, if the country lacks a sufficiently professional Weberian bureaucracy, this is no reason for not beginning public management reform: both reforms may be implemented at the same time. Developed countries already had competent senior civil services, and could proceed from that position.

---

[13] Still in 1998, the World Bank understood administrative reform as downsizing the state organization and completing civil service reform. At that time, its staff was just beginning to understand what was meant by public management reform, but not supporting it, based on the sequencing argument.

The fact that the sequencing hypothesis is often mistaken does not mean that developing countries should copy strictly the public management reforms adopted by developed countries. They will have to consider the specificities that they face, they will have to admit that clientelism or pork-barrel practices will be more widespread, that society will be less cohesive and that its moral standards may be different. In the case of the 1995 Brazilian public management reform, which was based on the British model, for instance, several adaptations were introduced by the local reformers. The role of senior civil servants at the strategic core of the state received more attention, their salaries were increased, yearly public entrance examinations were established for all state careers[14], and the role of auditing was not underestimated, although auditors were asked to pay more attention to outcomes than to procedures. Training of senior and middle-level civil servants received priority. In other words, there is no reason why a developing country cannot continue to build its professional public administration while, at same time, it starts to implement public management reform.

One of the major advantages that developing countries enjoy, besides the possibility of copying technologies, is the capacity to 'import' institutions. International organizations insist on exporting institutions and reforms, but such exports often fail because they are not adapted to local conditions. Importing institutions is quite different, because it implies ownership of the institutions being imported by nationals who will be able not only to adapt them to local conditions but also to commit people – other senior civil servants and society in general – to the new rules of the game. Commitment to new institutions does not follow automatically from ownership of the reform by nationals, but it is a condition for it. What is certain is that institutional reforms – and public management is nothing more than a set of institutions – are effective only when, besides being well designed and adapted to real conditions, they are ingrained in the social texture of a nation.

Conclusion

We began this essay by asking what kind of public administration reform in developing countries would contribute to economic development and the achievement of the United Nations' MDGs. After describing a model of public management reform called the structural public governance model, we argued, first, that it made the state more capable and more efficient in so far as it adopted a particular

---

[14] Previously, only the diplomacy and the military careers had yearly entrance examinations.

structure of division of labor between the state organization itself; public, non-state; corporatist and private organizations; and adopted a managerial strategy which, by making senior civil servants more autonomous and more accountable, motivated them and allowed them to be more efficient. Second, it was argued that, in so far as the state is the key instrument of collective action at a nation's disposal for promoting its economic development, making it more capable certainly would make governments more effective in defining, along with society, a national strategy of growth. Third, the sequencing thesis, which maintains that, if a developing country had not completed its bureaucratic or civil service reform, it can not undertake public management reform was rejected. There is no reason why a country can not undertake or continue civil service reform while gradually implementing public management reform.

In reality, developing countries can be divided into middle-income and low-income categories. Without question, middle-income or intermediate developing countries are able to import institutional reforms and innovations and profit from that. What is dangerous is for them to accept uncritically exported institutions which often do not take account of their national interests. In relation to poor countries, however, the problem is more complex, and more doubts than certitudes are the advisable attitude. More than other countries, they need above all else to build a strong, capable state, because a reasonably well-structured and relatively corruption-free state is a condition for their profiting from the aid that they receive from rich and middle-income countries. Indeed, the program that the United Nations organized to channel aid to poor countries is based on the assumption that some of those countries have already met such minimum conditions.

The UN Millennium Project's main document (2005) asserts that 'it is the responsibility of countries themselves to strengthen their own government systems'. It divides poor countries into those headed by 'rapacious government leadership' and those provided with 'well intentioned governments', and proposes that developed countries direct 0.7 % of their GDP to aid the latter group of countries.[15] In any case, poor countries have no alternative but to try to build state capacity. To achieve that, they should resist financing growth with additional international indebtedness, because growth comes out of domestic not

---

[15] UN Millennium Project (2005): 113-114. The Millennium Project was commissioned by the United Nations Secretary-General in 2002 to develop a concrete action plan for the world to abolish the grinding poverty, hunger and disease affecting billions of people. It is an independent advisory body headed by Jeffrey Sachs. See also Sachs (2005).

foreign savings.[16] And they should be critical of the recommendations and conditionalities that usually come together with aid. With these caveats, the structural public governance model, well adapted to their realities, will be a good institution to import.

References

Bresser-Pereira, Luiz Carlos (2004a) *Democracy and Public Management Reform*. Oxford: Oxford University Press.

Bresser-Pereira, Luiz Carlos and Peter Spink, eds. (1999) *Reforming the State*: *Managerial Public Administration in Latin America*. Boulder, Co.: Lynne Rienner Publishers.

Bresser-Pereira, Luiz Carlos and Yoshiaki Nakano (2002) "Economic growth with foreign savings?" Paper presented at the Seventh International Post Keynesian Workshop, Kansas City, Mi., June 28-July 3 2002. Available in the original at www.bresserpereira.org.br, and, in Portuguese (Revista de Economia Política 22(2) April 2003: 3-27). A181

MARE (Ministry of Federal Administration and Reform of the State) (1995) *White Paper on the Reform of the State Apparatus* (*Plano Diretor da Reforma do Aparelho do Estado*). Brasilia: Imprensa Nacional, November 1995. Available in English in www.bresserpereira.org.br.

Pollitt, Christopher and Geert Bouchaert (2000) *Public Management Reform*. Oxford: Oxford University Press.

Ranson, Stewart and John Stewart (1994) *Management for the Public Domain*. London: The Macmillan Press.

Sachs, Jeffrey (2005) *The End of Poverty: Economic Possibilities for Our Time*. New York: Penguin Press.

Silberman, Bernard S. (1993) *The Cages of Reason*. Chicago: Chicago University Press.

UN Millennium Project (2005) *Investing in Development: A Practical Plan to Achieve the Millennium Development Goals*. London and Sterling, VA: Earthscan.

---

[16] On the critique of growth *cum* foreign savings strategy in the last years, see Bresser-Pereira and Nakano (2002).

Aligning the Agenda on the Role of the African State in Achieving Africa's Development Goals: Africa in the Work of the UN CEPA (2003- 2005)

by

*Geraldine J Fraser-Moleketi**

The term of the first Committee of Experts on Public Administration (hereafter, the Committee or CEPA) ran simultaneously with many interesting initiatives and interventions in the domain of public governance and administration. It functioned against the backdrop of the Millennium Development Declaration and Goals (MDGs) as well as a growing concern about the effects of globalization and the changing post 9/11 international agenda on security and international terrorism. In Africa, the context was shaped by the emergence of The New Partnership for Africa's Development (NEPAD) from the New African Initiative (NAI) and its predecessor processes – the Millennium Partnership for African Recovery Programme (MAP) and the OMEGA plan. These were essentially put forward by a new generation of African leaders who saw the importance of democracy and sound governance for the realization of development on the African continent.

The Committee functioned in a period during which the Washington Consensus drew serious criticism, sometimes from former insiders of the system; at other times from more expected quarters, such as global social movements. Structural adjustment as a concerted effort to secure certain types of economic and associated governance reforms in developing countries became increasingly discredited. Essentially all of these developments, as well as many others, allowed for a re-thinking of the role of the state and the role of public administration in supporting the state to fulfill its role.

---

* Minister for Public Service and Administration, Republic of South Africa and a member of the Committee of Experts on Public Administration of the United Nations.

Introduction

The influence of the adoption of the UN Millennium Development Declaration on re-establishing the importance of the "public" interest and domain after a period in which the dominant trend was to turn to the "private" and letting concern for individual interests dominate should not be underestimated. World leaders accepted the collective responsibility reflected in the Declaration to uphold the principles of human dignity, equity and equality on a global and national level. The Declaration chose to define "freedom" not in the typical liberal way by emphasizing the rights of the individual, but rather defined the concept in terms of public and collective concerns: freedom from hunger, freedom from fear of violence, repression and injustice and freedom from living in an ecologically destroyed environment. The Declaration supports this by adopting an orientation that recognizes the importance of solidarity as a vehicle to distribute burdens and costs in line with social justice and equity principles. Viewed from this perspective the Declaration opened the way to engage critically with some of the worst legacies which the neo-liberal agenda has left in the public administration domain, i.e. the "privatization" of public issues and, in the process, the negation of the role of the state.

Notwithstanding severe criticism regarding some of the outcomes of public sector reform in terms of the neo-liberal agenda, given the widespread support for its public administration manifestation, the New Public Management (NPM) and the fact that it is still widely embraced in the literature and taught at academic institutions, it is not surprising that the Committee during the period got caught up in something of a conceptual Tower of Babel. Thus, different experts held different perceptions as to the utility of NPM for the way forward and to bring about the necessary reform program that will support the implementation of the MDGs and other development goals. In reporting the work of CEPA, this divergence was accommodated through carefully crafted statements such as:

> "the more successful aspects of new policies such as NPM, should be adopted, adapted, evaluated and applied within the constraints of the differing levels of development, the exigencies of different societies and political systems and the characteristics of the public administration systems to which they are applied, while

correcting excesses that are incompatible with the nature of public service." (report of UN CEPA 2004: 3)

These weaknesses have emerged and are the predictors of the direction of the change that we are currently seeing. We know that we are in the process of making a paradigm adjustment – maybe this time a little bit more balanced and, somewhat more sophisticated in allowing for differentiation and the influence of specific regional and national contexts. Nevertheless, changes to public administration is in the process of taking place. That does not mean that all changes that came with NPM will be erased. Traces, even more than traces, of those changes that were functional will survive and will form part of the heritage of the subject area. But aspects, such as those that undermine the role of the state as key force in development, will be displaced by new initiatives, new concepts, and so forth. Therefore, changes that have occurred in public administration are natural and could have been expected and so are the ones that are currently in the making.

This paper sets out to document how Africa featured in the work of the CEPA during 2002- 2005. It further comments on how the thinking advanced in the UN CEPA during this period harmonizes with the latest initiatives on the African continent. For a summary on the issues covered by the various CEPA meetings, see diagram 1. In this regard the paper will make special reference to the re-emergence of the idea of the "strong state" as a necessary pre-condition for sound governance relations with the private sector and civil society – all in the interest of human development and economic growth. It will also reflect on the importance of partnerships as an important form of governance relations.

Diagram 1: UN CEPA Meeting Themes (2002 – 2005)

1ST MEETING	2ND MEETING	3RD MEETING:	4TH MEETING
Themes: Critical Role of Public Administration and Good governance in implementing the UN Millennium Declaration: •Institutional Capacity; •Human Resource Development; •Financial Capacity; and •Knowledge, Innovation and Technological capacity •Launch of the first World Public Sector Report: Globalization and the State	Themes: •Status and Trends in E-Government Development •Strategies for High Quality Staffing in the Public Sector •Mainstreaming Poverty Reduction Strategies within the Millennium Development Goals: the Role of Public Administration	Theme: Revitalization of Public Administration •The Role of Human Resources in Revitalizing Public Administration •Role of the Public Sector in Advancing the Knowledge Society •Strengthening Public Administration for the MDGs – a Partnership Approach Public Sector Institutional Capacity for African Renewal	Theme: Revitalizing Public Administration •Emerging issues in revitalizing Public Administration •Bottom-up approach and methodologies for developing foundations and principles of sound Public Administration •Promoting and Rewarding Innovation and Excellence for Revitalizing Public Administration and Service Delivery Roundtable with ECOSOC
2002	2003	2004	2005

Africans in CEPA and Africa in the Work of CEPA

During the period under review, CEPA has consistently given prominence to Africa – both in terms of process, as well as in substantive discussion. Six members of the committee for 2002 – 2005 hailed from Africa. They represent a good variety of African regions – Northern, Southern, Eastern and Western Africa. In addition the composition reflects the diversity of colonial experiences with the British, French, Spanish and Portuguese colonial histories notable in the countries of origin of the different members. Compared to the members from other parts of the world, political lineage in current and previous appointments, rather than career public service or academic expertise features more prominently.

Africans were entrusted with many of the leadership roles in the CEPA. Prime Minister Apolo Nsibambi from Uganda was elected at the start of the first session as Chairperson for the Committee for the period 2002 – 2005. It was only in 2003, due to his inability to attend the meeting that the position of Chair reverted to one of the Vice Chairpersons, Madame Bourgon from Canada (UN CEPA, 2003). For the 2nd to 4th meetings of the CEPA the Rapporteurship also rested on an African, Prof. Oscar Monteiro. On average four out of the six African members attended the four meetings of the CEPA. Unfortunately one member was never in a position to take up his seat.

Some would argue that Africa featured disproportionately strongly in the reports and resolutions that emanated from CEPA over the period. The very first report of the Committee contains a recommendation that, given the special needs of Africa, a special focus in terms of support and technical and professional assistance should be made available to Africa and that the UN should in its activities take into account the partnership approach advocated by the New Partnership for Africa's Development (NEPAD) (UN CEPA 2002). These sympathies were subsequently formally endorsed by the 45th plenary meeting of ECOSOC (E/Res/ 2002/40).

It was, however, during the second and subsequent sessions that Africa really became prominent. A recommendation was made to ECOSOC to include a separate point on Africa for the third session of UN CEPA, under the theme *"Public Sector Institutional Capacity for African Renewal"*. This was done in response to the United Nations Millennium Declaration and in order to promote public sector institutional capacity for African renewal. By dedicating a separate discussion point to Africa, the secretariat was effectively instructed to commit a substantial chunk of its analytical and other resources to develop a dedicated background paper on the issue of institutional capacity building in Africa. In

46

addition, the Committee also urged the Secretariat to undertake, together with national and regional organizations, a systematic assessment of institutional capacity requirements in sub-Saharan Africa, and produce a compendium and compilation of experiences and good practices in public administration. This would provide the empirical basis for engaging with the institutional capacity constraints in Africa.

The second meeting further recommended that the UN Secretariat should make a special effort in terms of African leadership development and specifically to support capacity-building and the development of partnerships with regional and national institutions to provide the necessary training. To this effect, a suggestion was made that the May 2003 meeting of the African Ministers that was to take place in Cape Town, South Africa be used to discuss the leadership development programme in Africa and to finalize the training programme and its modalities. The African Ministers duly responded to this and in 2005 this initiative received further impetus when under the aegis of the African Ministers' Conference, the African Management Development Institution Network (AMDIN) was formally launched. UN DESA played an important role throughout the formation of AMDIN and was also present at the AMDIN launch in August 2005 in Sandton, South Africa.

As per the 2003 recommendation, the agenda for the third meeting did include a dedicated discussion on Africa's institutional capacity. This resulted in a recommendation put forward to member states in Africa that they should take the following measures to strengthen their institutional capacities:

- Implement the Governance and Public Administration Programme of the African Union;
- Institute mechanisms for the implementation and dissemination of the Charter for the African Public Service;
- Adopt methods, processes and systems, such as decentralized governance, that foster opportunities for popular participation in the governance and development process;
- Strengthen the law-making, oversight and budget review capacities of the legislature;
- Depoliticize the public service and transform it into a professional and non-partisan, but politically sensitive, agent; and
- Strengthen the judiciary to ensure predictability and peaceful resolution of disputes arising out of trade, industrial and international relations (UN CEPA, 2004: p16).

The recommendations of the third meeting also strongly show the reciprocity in the relations between Africa, the CEPA and the UN generally, but specifically UN DESA. Recommendation 7 that was directed at the UN asks that the UN system should continue providing substantive technical and advisory support aimed at strengthening governance and public administration institutions in African States. It should also assist the secretariat of NEPAD in implementing the Governance and Public Administration Programme for Africa as was approved by the African Ministers Conference held in 2003, and subsequently adopted by the AU. It calls for further assistance with the implementation of regional integration and research and information dissemination support (UN CEPA 2004: 17).

Strong State and Capacity Development

Notwithstanding significant political and economic reform efforts in Africa since the late 1980s, recent assessments are quite pessimistic regarding its effects - specifically the sustainability of efforts where some initial successes have been demonstrated. The single most important factor that has been identified to cause such poor performance in Africa is the weak state of the public sector and the institutions of governance (Kayizzi-Mugerwa, 2003: 1; Mbaku 2000: 2).

The importance of sound public administration practice and capable public governance institutions for development is by now well established and widely recognized (NEPAD, 2001: 5; Wilson et al. 2001; UN CEPA 2005). The Rapporteur's Report of the 4th Pan African Conference of Ministers of Public Service also reflects on this theme, starting off with the statement that state capability is critical for creating the necessary conditions for development, promoting economic growth and implementing poverty reduction programmes (NEPAD, Undated, p. 5).

The African Ministers Conference finds itself part of a more general pattern of thinking. Note, for example, in this regard the statement by the 2002 Public Administration and Development resolution that was adopted by ECOSOC, *reiterating that:*

"...efficient, accountable, effective and transparent public administration, at both the national and international levels, has a key role to play in the implementation of the internationally agreed goals, including those contained in the United Nations Millennium Declaration, and in that context stresses the need to strengthen national public sector administrative and managerial capacity-building, in particular in developing countries and countries with economies in transition (UN E/ Res/2002/40);

The Report of the fourth meeting of CEPA regarding the public sector institutional capacity for African renewal however, said it all. It reports:

"The Committee noted that developing institutions of governance and public administration in Africa was critical in responding to the momentous challenges of achieving the Millennium Development Goals in general, and poverty eradication and sustainable development in Africa in particular. Without overcoming obstacles in governance and public administration, Africa will continue to lag behind in the achievement of the Millennium Development Goals." (UN CEPA 2004: 9)

Bearing in mind the need for quality and sound administration, it should come as no surprise that the African Union chose to emphasize the importance of capacity development in the theme it identified for its first decade in operation, i.e. Decade For Capacity Building In Africa. This emphasis has been supported and mirrored by the attention that has been given to the theme of capacity building during the past few years by many of the important international policy "think tanks" on governance related issues. The biggest testament to this emphasis is the work of CEPA itself. The human resource focus has been an annual feature for the CEPA meeting since its inception, and has featured very strongly in the first World Public Sector Report, as well as in the 2005 version of the same report under the title Unlocking the Human Potential for Public Sector Performance.

Before getting deeper into this theme, one important issue must be noted. Writing about "the African State" -- be that weak or strong - as if it is a homogenous concept without pointing to the very different situations at the national, sub-regional and regional level, will be misleading. Great diversity is found across the 47 different states on the African continent. This is partly as a consequence of the different colonial histories, but the very powerful role of a rich tapestry of ethnic diversity also should not be ignored. Similarly, the recency of the democratization experience should not be underplayed. As peace initiatives across Africa are starting to bear fruit, the challenges for building and strengthening public administration across the continent is growing.

Many of the countries emerging from decades of internal strife have to start with the very basic activities of establishing who actually constitute their civil services and determining the capacity they can draw on. They have to re-establish the most basic of administrative systems, such as archives and record-keeping. By no stretch of the imagination can this be deemed to be administrative reform, since there exists very little to reform. It is not re-engineering, because there was little engineered before. When people are critical about Africa's progress with establishing effective administrations, they must bear in mind that many of these countries are still in a war situation, or very newly emerged from situations of deeply entrenched conflict.

Recognizing the degree of diversity found across the continent should lay to rest the misunderstanding that Africa is a single entity, rather than a vast continent. It is this diversity that militates very strongly against a "one size fits all" approach in terms of public sector reform. Since 2001, the UN Group of Experts in Public Administration and Finance (predecessor of the UN Committee of Experts on Public Administration) and the Committee of Experts itself have strongly argued against this practice that has characterized the "New Public Management" paradigm (UN DESA, 2001: 55) – 59).

Diversity across African institutions of governance poses particular challenges for the harmonization of the public administration experience, as well as to any initiatives to strengthen regional and continent wide programmes. It further poses challenges to the issue of an emerging convergence and standardization of thought on what construes "good governance" and how these standards are being used and seen as the new set of "conditionalities" – once such a powerful tool in the hand of multilateral organizations that it effectively stunted the growth potential of Africa over many decades (Bretton Woods Project, UK - September 13, 2005).

The NEPAD founding document (NEPAD, 2001) identifies the weak state in many African countries as a major constraint on sustainable development. Consequently, it identifies one of the main challenges facing many African countries to be the need to strengthen the capacity to govern, as well as the ability to develop long-term policies.

During its first term, the CEPA also repeatedly referred to the need for a strong and capable state. The first World Public Sector Report was quite adamant in terms of setting this agenda. In later years, it seemed as if this point was more generally shared, although never unanimously and enthusiastically embraced by all CEPA members. The remarkable progress made in terms of this debate was the inclusion in the report of the third meeting of the CEPA that "the rollback of the State has been an inappropriate strategy" (UN CEPA 2004: 3) and the admission that "Public administration remains the pre-eminent locus and responsible guarantor of the public interest and of providing public service" (UN CEPA 2004: 4). More palatable were ideas relating to building the capacity of the state and its institutions. The compromise seemed to have centered on the idea of decentralized, rather than centralized capacity.

The author of this particular contribution consistently argued over the years, and through many interventions in the CEPA, that in the African context no other configuration of power than a strong state would have the necessary effect on our developmental agenda. Obviously such strength would not be to the exclusion of other strong and competent players, but it certainly is the sine qua non for the other sectors to also fully develop within the African context. If the capability in the state sector in Africa is circumscribed, so much more the situation in the other two critical sectors – market and civil society. Both are dependent on the state to pro-actively create an environment within which all can function to their full potential and play the roles for which they are traditionally most appreciated. In addition, it is important to keep in mind that the responsibility for regulation and performance management of NPM influenced outsourced arrangements will inevitably still be at the government level.

Regarding the debate on centralized vs. decentralized capacity, once again it can not be placed in an either/or context. What is at stake is the issue of the level at which governance aspects are dealt with most effectively and the issue of subsidiarity, i.e. that responsibility can only be devolved to a lower level if the requisite capacity exists to discharge that responsibility competently. Consequently, while in terms of thinking about democratic decision-making, a more local approach might therefore be preferred, in terms of service delivery and the rendering of many crucial public services in the developmental context, it might be better to use capacity found in national government departments, rather than to force the issue of decentralization as a matter of principle. In addition, macro co-ordination and commensurate monitoring and evaluation can only happen from the center of government – nowhere else.

What many post-conflict African countries currently must concentrate on in their initial phases of public administration construction is establishing the central capabilities of policy management, planning, budgeting, and human resource management as well as establishing civilian control over the security forces. This should not be interpreted as preoccupation with the centralization of power, but rather the situation should be regarded as a pragmatic one and comparable to other cases of post-war public service structuring and functioning, e.g. Germany and the USA post WWII. The position that African participants assumed at the 6th Global Forum on the Reinvention of Government regarding devolution of power and decentralization is that although the positive aspects of these are recognized, we are cautious. During the Africa preparatory meetings for the 6th Global Forum it was concluded "decentralization and devolution is fraught with a number of challenges, including the challenge of ensuring active integration between levels of government and the provision of resources for localised governance institutions".

The 2005 UN CEPA report contains a more qualified position on the issue of decentralization as compared to the resolution that was suggested by African governments. It states "... the matter of decentralization ought to be handled sensitively, for it need not always lead to a deepening of democracy." Clearly, Africa's contributions in this regard did contribute to a sharpening of the formulation and that this later position will be more beneficial in terms of taking governance forward in the African context.

The benchmark for public administration should not be merely the existence or even the size of the state machinery. Rather, the emphasis should be placed on the "soundness" and the capability of those institutions to bring to execution what the people and their representatives expect and need.

The "capacity" discussion is, however, a complex one. The literature on public administration in Africa suggests that bureaucracies play a "contradictory and conflict-ridden role" and that they are both cause and solution to Africa's problems (Kayizzi-Mugerwa, 2003). Mbaku (2000) advances a particularly interesting thesis, which departs from the more widely held opinion that Africa's problem can be attributed to capability related factors. He argues that many policy mistakes committed in Africa cannot be attributed to "incompetence, ill-informed and poorly educated but well-meaning policymakers" as the majority of analysts would like to argue, but they are in effect the result of deliberate and purposeful programmes promoted by opportunistic civil servants and politicians seeking ways to enrich themselves. Mbaku posits that post-colonial institutional arrangements in Africa enhanced the ability of opportunistic officials to capture state structures and abuse their positions at the cost of establishing an indigenous entrepreneurial class and creating much needed broad societal wealth to address the poverty problems faced by the continent and its people.

The CEPA therefore justifiably addressed the issue of ethical and clean government throughout the past four years. UNDESA has supported the development of the African Charter on Public Administration, one of the early products of the Conference of African Ministers on Public Administration and has subsequently held the existence of such a Charter up as a best practice to be emulated. CEPA has also specifically recognized the African initiatives in terms of implementing integrity, transparency and accountability programmes. Although not mentioned by name in the summary report, the African Peer Review Mechanism stands out in this regard.

It can safely be assumed that public administration in the context of pressing poverty and resource scarcity will be different from that in resource rich and infrastructurally well-endowed societies. Note, for example, the difference in availability and utilization of information and evidence to support decision-making processes. In addition, the democratic experience might also be very different, e.g. need for direct involvement vs. satisfaction with electronic engagement and more remote/ representative processes. It, however, definitely spills over to issues of the ability to attract highly skilled people and reward them adequately – thus, making available resources for ongoing human resource development.

State capacity can therefore not be discussed without making mention of the "African Brain Drain". This phenomenon has resulted in a depletion of needed expertise on the continent and recent trends suggest that nearly 20,000 trained intellectuals are annually leaving the continent for higher salaries and political stability in foreign countries (Cheru 2002: 253). When one learns about the fact that Niger only recently afforded their first salary increase for public servants in 25 years, the magnitude of the problem faced by African countries to retain their very necessary skills base for the public service truly begins to assume practical meaning (Reuters AlertNet, UK - September 18, 2005).

Challenges for the Next CEPA (2006-2009) in Respect of Africa

In summary, the discussion about state and state capacity has many dimensions and thus due regard needs to be given to the complexity of the issues, as well as the context - specific variation that underpins much of it. Not unexpectedly, a number of challenges for continued fruitful interaction between CEPA and the African agenda for public administration in the interest of development, poverty alleviation and wealth creation could be highlighted.

1. Whilst scholarship on African public administration has been on the increase, and the UN also contributes to publishing on the topic, it has been noted that the reports and publications – emanating from within UN structures as well as elsewhere - sometimes lack academic and empirical rigor. Strong assertions are sometimes made, whilst drawing on dated sources. For example, during the third session of CEPA, the background document on African institutional capacity used Tanzania as an example

to show the deterioration of purchasing power of civil service salaries. The source relied on, however, was a 1986 source, almost twenty years old.

One of the sources consulted in preparation of this study, Kayizzi-Mugerwa, draws on two 1997 resources (Aron 1997 and Rose-Ackerman 1997) to justify a point made in 2002 that "political exclusion tends to be the norm rather than inclusion" (Kayizzi-Mugerwa 2002). The public administration terrain in Africa is rapidly changing, with a large number of initiatives having been introduced over a very short space of time. The challenge would therefore be for analysts to remain absolutely current on the topic, as well as to continue strengthening both the quality and the volume of scholarly and practitioner outputs on the topic of African public administration.

2. The regional economic communities (RECs) have been clearly identified as the main planning, co-ordination and monitoring vehicles for the NEPAD programme of action. Consequently, public administration in regional organizations is becoming highly relevant. The African Ministers committee focused one of its input papers for the 2005 conference on this topic, but to a degree this move only signaled the start of the conversation in the African context on this extremely complex issue.

The CEPA 2002-2005 accepted the importance of the RECs in terms of leadership development and the broader capacity discussion (UN CEPA 2004: 10) A strengthened emphasis on this aspect will not constitute a deviation from the overall direction of the Committee, but rather will build upon an already established agenda. Other parts of the world, e.g. Europe, are well-steeped in these issues. Consequently, the CEPA might want to consider for inclusion on its future agenda more in-depth discussions and reflection on the inner-workings of these existing complex networks of administration that cut across national administrations, but also include partnerships across state, market and civil society boundaries.

3. During the operation of the first Committee, certain initiatives focused upon calling for the drafting of a single "Code" for public administrative practice and/or the drafting/ identification of common sound public administration principles (UN CEPA 2005: 15). The existence of the African Charter for Public Administration has on occasion been invoked

in support of this (UN CEPA 2003). On the other hand, there has been increasing recognition of the importance of our individual histories and contexts, especially in terms of how our institutional arrangements develop and manifest themselves.

As a result, we have walked away from the one-size-fits all approach that has dominated some thinking in public administration until very recently, and which produced a number of wrong roads in terms of public administration reform initiatives on the African continent. These included pressures to down-size public administrations where they were already inadequate, or outsourcing where the outsourcing partners were not strong enough to dispatch with their new undertakings. We have not yet entirely won this battle. Note, for example, the recent criticism of the World Bank for continuing to demand down-sizing of the public sector in order to qualify for loans – all of this under the cloak of advancing "good governance" (Bretton Woods Project, UK - September 13, 2005.)

During the existence of the next committee, we need to remain extremely cautious that the many attempts currently underway to construct indices of governance, measures of assessment to establish governance capability and the like, do not turn into new conditionalities that once again force us into the thinking of one standardized pattern as the template to which we all have to conform. If we fail in this, and fail to recognize that the liberal definition of democracy is not necessarily the most acceptable, and certainly not the only configuration of democracy – particularly in the view of Africans – Africa will once again suffer under a new set of "good governance" conditionalities, the outcome of which is likely to not be much different from those conditionalities suffered under in terms of structural adjustment.

Conclusion

The CEPA has during 2002 – 2005 taken forward and supported an agenda that highlighted Africa's challenges in terms of getting the necessary state machinery in place to give effect to both the NEPAD and MDG development goals. A strong relationship of reciprocity of influence and support has developed between the agendas and work of the CEPA, UNDESA and the African Ministers Conference on Public Administration – the body that is effectively responsible for the AU Programme on Public Administration. This relationship is likely to continue during the term of the second CEPA which will serve between 2006 and 2009. The composition of the second CEPA allows for sufficient continuity, while at the same time introducing some new thinking to the work of the Committee.

The road for Africa in terms of establishing and developing state machinery is a long one fraught with many obstacles and challenges. However, many exciting initiatives are underway which are deserving of encouragement and goodwill, as well as support in more substantive ways. The UN is but one agency that can play a continuing role in this regard. Although Africa can learn through the exchange of thinking, and some borrowing from international examples, she remains her own best learning laboratory. Africans should be given the opportunity to reflect on our own shortcomings and come up with corrective measures. Chinua Achebe, the eminent Nigerian novelist, author of *Things Fall Apart*, says that Nigeria, and for that matter Africa, has seen "the excesses of bad government which lie like a curse on the continent", but he also notes that these very nightmares will serve as correctives for the future. "We're not good students, but in the end we do pick up pieces here and there. This is the hope, the only hope, perhaps" (Quoted in Pahad 2002).

References

Bretton Woods Project 13 September 2005 "United Kingdom Cuts Through World Bank Spin on Conditionality"

Cheru, F (2002) African Renaissance: Roadmaps to the Challenge of Globalization. London: Zed Books

Kayizzi-Mugerwa, S (2003) (ed.) Reforming Africa's Institutions: Ownership, Incentives and Capabilities. United Nations University Press, New York.

Mbaku, John M. 2000. "Governance, Wealth Creation and Development in Africa: The Challenges and the Prospects" African Studies Quarterly 4(2): 1. [online] URL:

NEPAD (Undated) Governance and Public Administration Programme. Pretoria, South Africa.

NEPAD (2001) The New Partnership for Africa's Development (NEPAD).

Pahad, A (2002) Foreign policy challenges facing SA in 2002: A year of defining moments in Africa's History, http://www.anc.org.za/ancdocs/pubx/umrabulo/umrabulo15/policy.html accessed 9/11/2002.

Reuters AlertNet, UK - September 18, 2005. Niger Civil Servants Get First Pay Rise in 25 Years

UN (2002) The critical role of public administration and good governance in implementing the United Nations Millennium Declaration: institutional capacity development. Report of the Secretariat

http://unpan1.un.org/intradoc/groups/public/documents/un/unpan003535.pdf

UN CEPA (2002) Report of the first session of CEPA (22-26 July 2002) to the Economic and Social Council. Official Records 2002 Supplement No. 24 (E/2002/84 – E/CN 16/2002/8)

UN CEPA (2003) Report of the second session of CEPA (7- 11 April, 2003) to the Economic and Social Council. Official Records 2003 Supplement No. (E/2003/44 – E/C.16 /2003/6)

UN CEPA (2004) Report of the third session of CEPA (29 March – 2 April 2004) to the Economic and Social Council. Official Records 2004 Supplement No. 44 (E/2004/44 - E/C.16/2004/9)

UN CEPA (2005) Report of the fourth session of CEPA (4 – 8 April 2005) to the Economic and Social Council. Official Records 2005 Supplement No. 24 (E/2005/44 - E/C.16/2005/6)

Wilson, F, Kanji, N and E Braathen (Eds.) (2001) Poverty Reduction: What Role for the State in Today's Globalized Economy? CROP International Studies in Poverty Research, Zed Books, London.

In Search of the Meeting Point Between the Necessary State and the Real Society: A Southern African Perspective

by

José Oscar Monteiro[*]

To speak of the state in Africa generally and, in particular, in Southern Africa, implies a new reading, a breaking up or relativisation of the concepts used about the state up to now. We must distinguish the modern state from other forms of endogenous organization.

The modern state has its historical beginnings in most of Africa as the colonial state[1] . This was an external state, or rather the local excrescence of a European state from which it took only some of its characteristics, as a rule those that were useful for the requirements of the moment. Its manifestations ranged from stopping points on the coast, to the trade in rare goods in Europe; from the slave trade, to the granting of vast territories to the crown companies. It culminated in the apparently effective occupation of territory as a result of the "reflex colonization" dictated by the Berlin Conference –a meeting of countries feeling the pressure of going through the industrial revolution[2].

In the phase following occupation of the territory, the colonial administration, as an external administration, was mostly interested in the sectors where the colonizer might benefit from its action – which meant development of the modern economy and the implantation of settlers. The regions most distant from the major coastal and commercial centres were a kind of secondary zone where the administration, apart from functions of authority, played only those roles which sporadically served the modern economy – labour recruitment,

---

[*] Professor, Witwatersrand University, South Africa, Coordinator of Project ISAP — Instituto Superior da Administração Pública, Mozambique, and former member of the Committee of Experts on Public Administration of the United Nations.
[1] This present argument is based essentially on the experiences of the two southern African states that speak Portuguese, given their distinct historical situation when compared to the other countries of the region.
[2] The _expression « reflex colonization » comes from Perry Anderson, *Le Portugal et la fin de l'ultracolonialisme*, Ed. Maspero, Paris, 1961

public works that connected areas of the modern economy, and pacifying resistance.

One notes that there are no broad, well-defined spaces that correspond to these distinctions, because the two forms of occupation, the modern and the peripheral, could co-exist in the same geographical zone. The distinction between "concelhos" (councils) and "circunscricoes" (circumscriptions) to some extent reflected this difference. Circumscription Administrators and Heads of Posts were appointed to manage the peripheral areas, with the job of slotting the population into the system. Representatives of traditional authorities were integrated, less as representatives of the population, than as agents of the administration, which resulted in placing them on the lowest rung of the colonial administrative hierarchy. One notes that this process was relatively recent: in substance - it only began at the end of the 19th century.

The result of this process is not a coherent state, but an apparently homogenous structure at the top, coexisting at the grass roots with a multiplicity of local situations. Some of these were situations where the colonial occupation was most evident – namely in the areas serving the modern economy. In others, where the costs of occupation were too large or out of proportion to the results obtained, authority was exercised by private companies endowed with sovereign powers (the crown companies). These situations often were coexisting with ones where the modern state was simply not present, where there were no public forces or private agents interested in it. As a backdrop, in all these situations, there is an underlying network of historical or natural leaderships of various kinds, more or less structured, more or less community based, but they are themselves evolving at varying paces depending on both endogenous and exogenous factors.

The inherited state is thus at the same time an external state, a centralized state and a limp state. External because the process of forming the endogenous modern state did not cover the entire territory. The state erected since the colonial period, which was proclaimed at independence, has this strong external mark. It is centralized because its commands derived essentially from a centre, at first in the colonial metropolis, and later in the country's capital. It is limp because, despite the force of its declarations, its real presence never extended over the entire country.

Unification, Homogenization and Re-Legitimation of the State

The eruption of nationalism, and the particular conditions of liberation, led to two important results – on the one hand, the development of certain experiences of social and state organization of a participatory nature, and, on the other, the end of colonial rule and the proclamation of an independent state.

The model adopted in the post-independence period tried to incorporate these two realities – a modern state of an essentially exogenous matrix, into which an attempt was made to insert experiences gained during liberation. Vices and deformations were to be rooted out of the former, in the attempt to use the state as an instrument in the service of new goals. Furthermore, the declared objective was to extend the action of the modern state to ever deeper levels of society, so as to combat the shortcomings, particularly in education and health, viewed as the major demands and the great priorities.

At first sight, the fascination that the modern state exercises on the generation that fought for independence may seem paradoxical. But this fascination can be understood by viewing the modern state as a priority instrument for undertaking rapidly the projects that embodied independence, because of its effectiveness, modernity and inclusiveness. From this point of view the experience of the states that emerged from the success of the liberation struggles of the 1970s does not differ from that of other African independences.

As assets in this process of building the modern state, we may include the stabilization of states, the surprising unanimity in affirming and defending the existing borders, the immense training efforts, the development of regulation and, in the first phase of all independences, undeniable successes in extending social services, particularly education and health. The case of the new states that emerged in the 1970s is paradigmatic from this viewpoint. The efforts undertaken after independence made it possible to extend literacy and health care to large percentages of the population, despite the serious organizational inadequacies of the system – and all of this took place in the framework of a policy of participation that was sustained over a long period of time.

It cannot be said that this state, as was desired at one time, achieved the objective of serving the formation of the Nation: the construction of national unity, understood as the identification of all citizens with the same flag, the same motherland, is not yet complete. Although it is not opposed, it is not part of daily life. In Angola and Mozambique, where long years of war interrupted essential overland communications, the idea of belonging to a larger whole still means little to broad strata of the population, and the specific factors for unification – schools, public service, a common language – are still not very present.

Still more important, it has been forgotten to assess rigorously whether a replica of the European state, imperfect and degenerate when applied in the colonies for the mere purpose of serving economic domination, was fully adapted to the new objectives.

A Better Process of Extension or a New Approach

The construction of the state in other parts of the world was undertaken by the territorial expansion of constituted powers, mergers and alliances between communities, and the deliberate extension of common values in an initial phase, in order to shift later to decentralization. The state in Africa did not follow this path. It appeared from above, supposedly already made.

In the period immediately following independence, and the same remains true today, the state was the mechanism available to carry out the objectives proposed for governance – namely carrying through economic goals, social well being, the legal security of citizens, and development policies in general.

In the current epoch, our states thus find themselves faced with a dual necessity: on the one hand, to strengthen and consolidate the modern state, and to integrate the inherited state with a strong external component of a western and particularly Portuguese type.

But while the modern state is a necessary, and probably the most appropriate path to the development process that locates the country within the concert of nations, and from which it cannot be removed on pain of marginalization, it is not sufficient. A strategic question is posed: to know whether it is essentially a matter of improvement, by extending the modern state more effectively or whether it is also a case of seeing another basis for the *res publica* in the roots of local social organization. This perception has been felt for more than a decade: an initial response was to seek greater approximation between the state and its citizens. This is the movement of decentralization.

Decentralization in the broad sense has two components: the decentralization and the deconcentration of modern structures. The first may take the form of municipalization through the creation of local authorities regarded as autonomous collectivities persons of a particular population and territory, which elect their leadership bodies – consisting as a rule of an assembly, a mayor, and a council. Proper decentralization involves the allocation of terminal powers to the local authority, recognizing that it is empowered to impose municipal taxes, and fix fees for services provided.

Deconcentration consists of attributing growing decision making powers to the representatives of the central administration, who are placed at the various rungs into which that central authority is broken down.

Both help increase participation, or facilitate consultation with the interested parties. Both appear in recent history as part of modern institutions: in the case of deconcentration because the deconcentrated structures are an integral part of the modern state and suffer from the same deficit of identity; in the case of decentralization, because this is often conceived of as the application or adaptation of an abridged model, sometimes inspired in the Portuguese archetype of "concelhos" (Councils). But lessons have not been drawn from the history of these bodies as regards what is valid within them as institutions born from growing communities of interest between citizens (the "neighbors") around shared historical experiences, concrete problems faced, and common interests to be defended.

What's Going on in the Rural Areas?

Solutions designed for the rural areas nowadays involve recognition that there is something that the modern state does not understand, that a way will have to be found of doing things that is different from that used in urban or peri-urban societies.

The reflection made so far has consisted essentially in proposing the recognition or enthronement of the local authorities, as a rule reduced to a chief, with some variants – traditional chiefs or other kinds of chieftainships.

The stress has sometimes been put on the person of the leader. This form of broaching the problem – common to both governments and oppositions –

seems to have been dictated mostly by the desire to pacify inter-group conflicts, for electoral motives, or in search of political support, rather than from a genuine recognition of the value and potential of the social and organizational realities of these local communities. It has its advantages and may even, in the long term, spark off new dynamics.

But it runs the risk of treating as instruments these "chiefs" who, in exchange for greater or lesser stipends and the use of the paraphernalia of power, are becoming auxiliaries of the administration in carrying out the functions of the modern state – collecting taxes, censuses, control of the population, and owners of electoral "corrals", as indeed some of the defenders of this kind of "recognition" of electoral authorities naively admit – rather than autonomous representatives of the communities, as was initially intended.

Is this the only possible response? It seems there is another path. That path is to look at rural society, look at the communities where people live as entities that have shown an ability to solve their own problems. To look at this society in its richness and problem solving capacity is to be made aware of its differences in terms of needs and rhythms of development which we should not try to force into uniformity with our own vision of progress. Rather, we should know how to recognize its capacities and its institutional value. In other words, the struggle against poverty begins by identifying the wealth that has been ignored.

Social Capital

Such a path means knowing and recognizing the forms of social organization at work in society, the valuing of the social capital that the forms of organization constitute and through which populations are structured. In the difficult years of the war, when the presence of the modern state disappeared, the populations survived either because they put together their own mechanisms of organization for survival and subsistence, or because of reconstructed rituals, such as the reconciliation rites reinvented that made it possible to end the traumas of a lacerating conflict. History put both Mozambique and Angola in the forced situation of making a capacity for self-organization emerge, which has won the right to citizenship and is based on the purest line of civic participation. The option will not be so much one of creating as one of recognizing and integrating. It is an historical occasion that should not be wasted. We are talking of a level which is both territorial and human, which is that of the communities through which the population is organized; when competence, the capacity to act and effectiveness are all the greater, the closer they are to the places where people live and work.

At the territorial level, this leads us to go beyond the more or less finished models of municipal decentralization and governmental deconcentration, and reach out to other realities, variable and sometimes even imperceptible, without names or insignia, but with proven capacity and willingness to organize, both in suburban areas and in the countryside, and join efforts to invert the situation of poverty that still persists there.

Subsidiarity

It may be asked whether this is not just a romantic over-estimation of the capacity of communities, such is their degree of de-modernization. It is soon understood that the term "communities", is not a homogenous idea, and neither is the notion of the African state or of states in general. There are differences in structuring, size and historical ballast.

Having said this, two arguments may be counter posed: the first is that what may be regarded as the "backwardness" of the communities' results from the fact that the modern state has concentrated in its own hands the main resources and the contacts with the modern world for decades. So it is not surprising that these communities at first sight seem unprepared to carry out certain activities that might very well be resolved at their level.

The second is that the notion of development is not the same as the standard metre deposited under vacuum in a western museum. Development is that which people desire at each moment to improve their lives, in the way that they understand, and at the pace they desire.

It is a matter of elementary justice that the state should return, or develop, these capacities. For example, up until now education has been exclusively within the competence of the state: the role of rural communities has been that of collaborating with the state by building premises in traditional material – but school management, the construction of modern buildings, the training of teachers: these all fall under the powers of the modern state. However, even if it seems obvious that teacher training, as well as curriculum – with a greater or lesser degree of adaptation, as regards knowledge of local reality and development – should remain concentrated in institutions at a territorial level higher than that of the community; the initiative to build schools, the decision on the type of construction – within pre-established quality and safety standards – and the hiring of building companies could be a task of the communities, in a process whereby their capacity is developed through the growing attribution of responsibilities.

It is becoming clear that, despite many well designed or generous efforts, the modern state will not be able to solve all of society's problems and needs. The communities are a necessary partner. It may even be asked whether the path followed so far, in making the communities mere formulators of demands, rather than executors of their own projects – is not one of the causes of the problem – powerlessness of the modern state, powerlessness of the communities!

State action should be undertaken within something similar to the principle of subsidiarity – recognizing achievements on the one hand, defining areas of competence and allocating part of the resources existing in the communities (land, natural resources such as forests, wild life, mineral wealth). This is an alternative to transferring everything to the modern state and hoping for a redistribution which is not only complex, but also risks falling hostage to the modern elites who control the state.

Parallel or Convergent Movements?

If a difference of substance between the modern state and the community is admitted, the question is posed of knowing how to approach these two moments in the construction of public institutions. There are two ways of implementation: in the first, the state would operate at two levels – one modern and the other traditional. These two aspects would coexist in their own worlds, they would have some moments of contact, but they would reflect two separate social realities, almost enshrining a duality of more or less well articulated statutes.

In the second approach, the two movements would be convergent: one movement from the top downwards corresponding to an extension of the modern state, and which would be expressed both in affirming the presence of the state as an instrument of representation and authority, as in the provision of essential public needs such as security and legal stability, the guarantee of basic rights and the corresponding provision of water, health and education services that legitimate the state in the eyes of citizens. The other movement would be from the bottom up, in which the communities see recognition granted to the ways of achieving public ends that they have been undertaking, and their capacity to provide more services of better quality is developed.

The desired result is a symbiosis which reflects today's complex reality – on the one hand the distance between two worlds, and on the other the mixing of urban, suburban and rural cultures which happens permanently but in an irregular way and at various paces, a symbiosis in which the forms of community social organization currently in force – real, functioning, recognized forms – are integrated into the state which modifies its external character without losing its potential of modernity. Thus, this unavoidable reality of the modern state will be renewed and revived through inflows from the real society.

Are These Not the Local Authorities of the Rural Areas?

If this is the case, will it not be this decentralization that allows the true meeting point between the state and society? Thus, the state will be pushed in the direction of all of society and not just those sectors either already integrated into the modern state – the urbanized and modernized social classes – or those which are now on its territorial or functional periphery – the suburban population. This problem is posed throughout southern Africa but its scale varies from country to country. In countries where there has been effective urbanization or suburbanization because of industrialization or voluntary or forced exodus from the countryside, the problem will be on a lesser scale. But in those states where the countryside represents a significant social reality, its stability involves the integration within it of social strata long left outside.

The Importance of the State-Community "Meeting Point"

But the problems of the local communities cannot be solved just at their level because they do not live in isolation. Alongside problems that can be decided upon and solved locally, there exist others where a solution can only be found at broader territorial levels. Thus, community development plans should be discussed at successively higher levels until they meet the planning movement from above. Note that here we are advocating not a process of extension guided from the top downwards, but two movements, one from above and the other from below. The important thing is to provide a moment which facilitates crossover between the two movements.

Such a process would contain several vectors, including:

1. a process animated by a deliberate will of the central government apparatus to transfer competences and decision-making powers to successively lower territorial levels, attentive to the nature of the activities, sector by sector, and always guided by the principle of preparing the ground for effective deconcentration/decentralization of action
2. a process of stimulating the poles of demand and making decision situated locally, that exercise pressure from the bottom upwards, forcing organizational change such as saying that it is the activity of the central administrative apparatus that must be adapted to needs and demands and not the other way round
3. requiring and determining responses to problems clearly identified by family and private producers and by the users of state services in general from both the central and local authority.

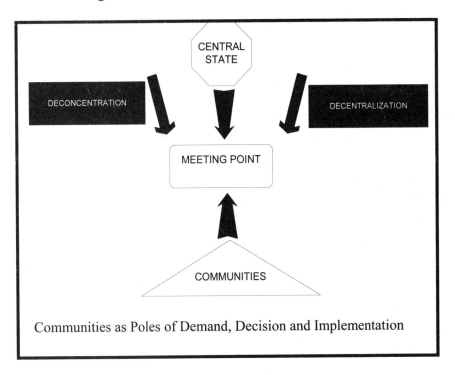

Communities as Poles of Demand, Decision and Implementation

A Revaluating of Traditional Functions

Given the present configuration of international society, which is based on the existence of states, the state is thus an unavoidable institution for the country's presence in the world. The usefulness of the modern state, regardless of its external origins and the criticisms that may be directed at it, is thus beyond discussion. Ideological excesses that led to rejecting as bad everything that was public and to disparage everything to do with the state, has sometimes, with the development of transnational crime, led either to the replacement of the state by mafias, or to reducing it to the servant of crime.

To carry out its function as an instrument of cohesion, the state should continue to undertake many of its traditional functions since it remains its duty to guarantee the security of citizens – since, in the formulation of Max Weber, the state continues to hold a monopoly on the legitimate use of force. Recent experiences, such as that of "community policing", in the Southern African region, show that even this task, which is traditionally an exclusive state responsibility, can be exercised with the collaboration of duly organized citizens; thus preventing situations of despair in which the population takes the law into its own hands.

But to handle the transition in this difficult period of uncertainty still more is needed: it is necessary to renew the pact of trust between citizens and the state, and this relies on three essential social factors: ethics, recognition of diversity, and participation.

Ethics: It is essential to win back credibility by restoring the ethical values of public service. States where school enrollment and the passing of exams are negotiated, where the providing of minimum health services by public establishments are seen as sources of benefits for those who control them, where public tenders are pre-determined to the benefit of those who hold power, where occupying a leadership position is seen as a passport to membership of the class of nouveaux riches, are on paths to disasters of an unpredictable scale. The attack on the state unleashed from other quarters for ideological reasons has served to legitimize its appropriation. In this sense, it is necessary "to de-privatize the state", to give value once more to phrases such as the ethics of public service, to rehabilitate the idea of avoiding conflicts of interest, to give content to declarations about the fight against corruption – all of which are at risk of becoming discredited.

Recognition of diversity: This implies abandoning the pure interpretation of the Jacobin myth of the homogenization and uniform modernization scarcely applicable to diverse societies. It postulates the recognition of diversities, but first of all they must be understood, so as not to become a prisoner of interest groups that may claim a monopoly on representing these groups or interests. From the nationalist experience in Southern Africa, there emerges the echo of a slogan, a movement launched by the Angolan nationalists in the 1950s – "Let's get to know Angola". To know and to recognize are today key words of a new public management that does not rely on books. They are the first steps towards a state that serves as a factor of national and social cohesion. This recognition of diversity – which we have been successively delaying because of the real and presumed risks that it contains – can be postponed no longer.

It is understood that such diversity makes it difficult to manage a modern kind of administration, which is keen on uniformity and simplicity both to make it possible to draw up clear and intelligible matrices, and also to favour the homogenous application of policies. This implies deliberately avoiding the attempt to impose norms through a uniform model. This will be a new effort, and sometimes will require a precursor, which implies the capacity to manage institutional diversity and to know how to deal with uncertainty.

Participation: Participation in this sense means incorporating the population into public matters through the already known mechanisms of deconcentration and decentralization. But participation should also mean incorporating the institutions of civil society with their characteristics of complementarity, criticism and dissent into public sector decision-making. These are critical forms of participation in societies – indeed, to dissent is the way in which many, if not most, people and groups participate. Societies are becoming ever more open as a result of the unstoppable circulation of information, but also in Southern Africa because of the efforts to generalize public education in which the first independence generation can justly take pride. Participation is transformed into a contribution if we know how to open doors and information to all groups anxious to make their civic contribution. To cite Kofi Annan, today's difficult times require something complex, but possible – Leadership with Empowerment.

Implementation of Universal
Primary Education in Uganda

By

*Apolo R. Nsibambi**

The Committee of Experts on Public Administration (CEPA), which was established in the year 2002 by the Economic and Social Council of the United Nations (UN) has since that time been meeting annually to discuss public administration matters related to implementation of the United Nations' Millennium Declaration. One such issue has been enhancement of the capacity of public administration to implement the UN Millennium Declaration. Those discussions have now generated what amounts to a potential framework for viewing the challenges of implementing the Millennium Declaration. That set of ideas is expected to enable member States to position themselves more strategically for carrying out this task.

Uganda was one of the one hundred, eighty-nine countries that adopted the Millennium Declaration during the Millennium Summit held in 2000. This declaration contained the Millennium Development Goals (MDGs) which constitute a development programme which the world community committed itself to achieve by 2015. These goals include numerical and time bound targets that express the achievement of fundamental aspects of human development. They are, therefore, derivates of the current human development paradigm of the world community.

In order to meet the realization of the Millennium Development Goals, the Government of Uganda is committed to:

i)   End armed conflicts, ensure security and provide a peaceful environment;

ii)   Promote good governance, transparency and accountability;

iii)   Play the leading role in mobilizing resources and coordinating key stake holders -- including communities, the private sector and development partners;

iv)   Allocate more resources to education, at least 2% of GDP;

---

* Past Chair person of the Committee of Experts on Public Administration of the United Nations and the Rt. Hon. Prime Minister of Uganda.

v)	Strengthen internal and external partnerships with various crucial players;
vi)	Enhance sub-regional and regional cooperation to promote the African Renaissance;
vii)	Create an enabling environment for full participation of women in leadership and other areas of development.

Seeking to illustrate the typical challenges facing the implementation of the Millennium Development Goals, this paper describes and analyses key experiences and issues that have characterized the implementation of Universal Primary Education (UPE) in Uganda. We shall review here, among other things, relevant background issues, a brief historical description of Uganda's education system, the critical factors that led to the adoption of UPE policy in Uganda, the main highlights of the UPE programme, the strategies formulated for its implementation, some of the key achievements it has registered, the challenges observed, the implications of the programme for post-primary education, and a look to the future, including an examination of the need to enhance the capacity of public administration to implement the Millennium Declaration. We conclude with some recommendations on what the UN could do to enhance capacity building to more effectively implement the Millennium Declaration.

Factors Leading to the Adoption of UPE

Uganda's Education system consists of pre-primary and primary school education; secondary education; teacher education; vocational, technical and business education (health, cooperatives, agriculture, veterinary) and tertiary education including university education and non-formal education. The primary education sub-sector is the largest with an enrollment of over seven million children.

The mandate of Uganda's Ministry of Education and Sports is to provide support, guide, coordinate, regulate and promote quality education to all persons in Uganda with the central objective of promoting national integration as well as integrating the individual citizen in national development. This acute perception of education as a key to national integration and prosperity gave strong impetus to Government's actions to review its past and present policy practices in the education sector. These reviews, briefly described below, have led to the development of the UPE policy and others that are bound to follow in the wake of implementing this policy.

71

Prior to the attainment of independence in 1962, the education system in Uganda was narrow and elitist and tended to alienate and exclude the majority of the citizens from participation. In order to redress the situation, the immediate post independence Government appointed the E.B. Castle Commission in 1963 to review the system and advise on a suitable education system for a newly independent country. The Commission recommended that there was need to expand primary education in order to meet the high level of demand for manpower created by the needs of a newly independent state.

In the short term, priority was given to secondary and post primary education in order to produce manpower that was urgently needed for economic development at that time. It was not until the period between 1972-1976 that concern was expressed about the neglect of primary education, which was then covering only 50% of the school-going age group. A more vigorous policy was proposed to overcome the deficiency in primary education by making it available to the rapidly increasing proportion of the school-going age group. This policy targeted achieving UPE by the year 2000.

In 1987, another Education Policy Review Commission (EPRC) was appointed. This Commission made recommendations, which were not implemented because of the political climate at that time. Indeed, the 1982-84 recovery programme, which aimed at making primary education available to all children, remained more of a wish than a reality because of the political turmoil that diverted resources from education to military operations.

It was not until 1987, during the rule of the National Resistance Movement, that the EPRC was reappointed to review the education system. It recommended policy reforms all the way from primary to tertiary education. The Commission further pointed out that primary education was the only formal education that most Ugandan children would ever receive. However, it also noted that primary education was the necessary foundation upon which subsequent education levels could be built and that it should therefore be given top priority.

Four years later, in 1991, the Government decided to implement measures designed to reverse the declining trends in the quality of education over the past two decades. In a policy statement contained in the "Background to the Budget, June 1991" the Government declared its sectoral strategy on primary education.

During the same year, the Government appointed a White Paper Committee to examine the EPRC report and identify the recommendations, which were acceptable and feasible to implement and make amendment where necessary. The Government White Paper Committee accepted the EPRC report on education and, in April 1992, the Government White Paper was published which contained all the approved reforms of the education system.

Consequently, a programme called the Primary Education Reform Program (PERP) was created and launched in 1993. The overall goal for PERP was to improve the quality and equity of primary education by:

(i)   Improving access and equity to basic education;
(ii)   Enhancing quality through training teachers;
(iii)   Strengthening capacity for education training and management;

In order to implement PERP, a project called the Primary Education and Teacher Development Project (PETPP) was designed as a trailblazer for achieving UPE, which was the ultimate goal.

The adoption of the new Constitution in 1995 provided a further impetus for introduction of more fundamental reforms for basic education in Uganda. In Article 30, the Constitution states. "All *persons have a right to education*". The Constitution also made it the obligation of the Government to provide basic education to its citizens; Article 30, Clause XVIII states thus;

The state shall provide free and compulsory basic education...
The state shall take appropriate measures to afford every citizen equal opportunity to attain the highest level of education standard possible.

Finally the Children's Statute of 1996 (Section 28) further emphasized the responsibility of the state in providing basic education by stating that; The child has a right to education and the state's duty is to ensure that primary education is free and compulsory.

Thus, a combination of factors that include global movements for basic education, a clear education policy framework, prioritizing basic education, and an elaborate legal framework all served to provide a conducive environment for introducing and implementing UPE in the Country. It was therefore not surprising that when the first direct election for the post of the President of the Republic of Uganda was taking place, President Museveni made it a platform issue and pledged to provide free primary education to four children per family. After being elected, the President acted to fulfil his pledge. He began by calling a national conference and announcing that the implementation of UPE was to begin in January of 1997.

Highlights of the UPE Programme

Aims and Objectives of UPE: Internationally, universal primary education is defined as the provision by the state of free *and compulsory* basic education to all children of school going age. In Uganda, however, UPE was initially defined as provision of basic education to four children per household. In the provision of this education, both the Government and the parents have costs and responsibilities to share. The Government obligation includes the mobilization of resources, paying tuition fees through capitation grant and the training of teachers, among other tasks. The responsibilities of the parents include providing scholastic materials, school uniforms and the basic necessities, including food.

As the programme unfolded, the definition of UPE had to be reviewed to reflect the changing circumstances. UPE is now defined as the provision of basic education to all Ugandan children of school going age. However, UPE in Uganda is not fully free because both the Government and the parents have financial obligations to meet in the education of the children. It is also not compulsory for parents to send their children to school, as there is no act of Parliament to make it mandatory. Moreover, some parents still may not be in a position to meet the irreducible minimum requirements.

The overall goal of UPE in Uganda is to increase *access*, *equity* and *quality* of primary education in Uganda. Its more specific objectives include:

(i)   Establishing, providing and maintaining quality education as the basis for promoting necessary human resource development

(ii)   Transforming society in a fundamental and positive way.

(iii)   Providing the minimum necessary facilities and resources to enable every child to enter and remain in school until the primary cycle of education is complete.

(iv)   Making basic education accessible to the learner and relevant to his or her needs -- as well as meeting national goals.

(v)   Making education equitable in order to eliminate disparities and inequalities.

(vi)   Ensuring that education is affordable by the majority of Ugandans.

By aiming to achieve UPE, Government is fulfilling its mission to eradicate illiteracy, while equipping every individual with the basic skills and knowledge with which to exploit the environment for both self and national development.

Design and Implementation Strategies: UPE was designed in 1997 as a national programme aimed at providing free education for four children per family. It was funded jointly by international development partners (funding agencies), the Government of Uganda and the local community. It is implemented by the local government. The programme had five components including: infrastructure provision, capitation grant, qualified teacher provision, primary school curriculum review and the provision of instructional materials. These were areas that were critical to providing basic education and total achievement of programme objectives.

Under the infrastructure development component, Government undertook to construct and furnish new facilities (i.e. classrooms, sanitary facilities and teachers' houses) and complete unfinished classroom buildings. Eighteen three-seater desks were provided to each classroom that was built. The objective of this component was to expand facilities to accommodate increased enrollments. In order to achieve this, Government set the following targets: one classroom for each 55 pupils; a ratio of one latrine per 40 pupils; and at least four teachers' houses per school. For schools in conflict areas, and other schools with special requirements, the Schools Facilities Grants (SFG) were made flexible enough to meet diverse needs.

With regard to Capitation Grants, Government undertook the responsibility of payment of tuition fees for four children per family there by relieving parents of the burden of payment of school fees. This guaranteed resources that were necessary for running school activities. These included extra instructional and scholastic materials, support of co-curricular activities, and the management of the school and its administration. The grant was targeted at only Government-aided primary schools and was computed annually as follows; 5,000 Uganda Shillings per pupil in P1-P3 and 8,100 per pupil in P4-P7. Beneficiaries of this grant included monogamous families, polygamous families, single parent families and orphans without parents.

It is the role of Government to provide adequate and qualified teachers for effective implementation of the programme. It is important to note that when UPE was announced, many children were newly attracted to school. Increasing enrollments therefore necessitated an increase in the number of teachers. Also, in order to improve the quality of instruction, there was a need to increase the qualifications of teachers. Government guaranteed funding for payment for additional teachers and for clearing salary arrears.

As part of the UPE program, a review of the primary school curriculum was undertaken. The review was aimed at making primary education relevant to the needs of individuals by equipping every individual with basic skills. The goal was to help develop functional literacy and numeracy, effective communication skills in local languages, appreciation of diversity in cultural practices, traditions and social organisations, and acceptance of a variety of social beliefs and values.

The Government set up a taskforce and subject panels to take the process forward. This resulted in producing two volumes containing the new curriculum. The first volume of the primary school curriculum includes four core subjects -- English language, integrated science, mathematics and social studies. The second volume contains, integrated production skills (IPS); Kiswahili and other language; music, dance and drama, physical education; and religious education.

Furthermore, Government undertook the responsibility to provide increased instructional materials. It was aimed at ensuring quality and equity through improving access and usage of scholastic materials. Instructional materials in primary schools include: core text books, teacher's guides, supplementary text books and basic teachers' professional references and pedagogic materials, pupils' basic reference books (Atlas and Dictionaries), supplementary reading books; and learning aids (specifically wall charts).

In 1993, there were 37 pupils for every book. In 2004, the ratio was 3 pupils to 1 book for primary three to primary seven core subjects. Children in primary one and two receive non-book materials. All this was possible because resources were made available through the Government recurrent budget for bulk purchases of these materials. The Ministry is now committed to ensure that these books are put in the hands of the pupils.

Finally, a number of complimentary programs and strategies have been adopted to consolidate the gains from UPE. These have been mainly in the area of Special Needs Education and Non-Formal Education.

Some of the Key Achievements of the Programme

According to Uganda's Poverty Reduction Strategy Paper (PRSP), primary education is among the basic requirements for a full life in the modern world. Therefore, basic education is one of the key strategies for poverty eradication in the Country. Government has, since early 1990, pursued policies intended to expand access to all levels of the education system with a special emphasis being placed on primary education which most directly benefits the poor.

In 1997, Universal Primary Education (UPE) was launched and has been being implemented since then. Its main objectives are to address inequality in the Country and improve the quality of life of its beneficiaries. Although UPE was initially meant for four (4) children per family, the policy was, as noted above, changed to target all school-going-age children. Clearly, the implementation of UPE has opened up the education space for children, especially of the poor, to access free education.

Today, eight years down the road, the education sector is one of the most successful sectors in Uganda in terms of the coverage and impact of its service delivery. The main achievement of UPE has been a surge in gross enrollment in primary schools. At the end of 1996, there were only 3 million registered primary school children, this figure has more than doubled and now stands at over 7.3 million. This, in turn, has meant significant increases in the number of teachers, text books and the like. These trends of growth are shown in Table 1 below.

Table 1: Growth in the Primary Sub Sector 1996-2004, as a Consequence of UPE

Year	1996	1997	1998	1999	2000	2001	2002	2003	2004
Male enrollments in all primary schools	1,647,742	2,832,472	3,061,722	3,301,888	3,395,554	3,528,035	3,721,135	3,872,589	3,721,911
Female enrollments in all primary schools	1,420,883	2,471,092	2,744,663	2,986,351	3,163,459	3,372,881	3,633,018	3,760,725	3,632,838
Total enrollment in all primary schools	3,068,625	5,303,564	5,806,385	6,288,239	6,559,013	6,900,916	7,354,153	7,633,314	7,354,749
Primary Schools	8,531	8,600	9,916	10,597	11,578	13,219	13,332	13,353	13,239
Number of teachers	81564	89247	99237	109733	110366	127038	139484	145587	145,819
Number of classrooms	25,676	25427	28380	43174	50,370	60,199	69,900	73,104	79,132
Core textbooks procured	783,556	2,112,104	1,492,186	1,331,710	1,171,235	2,086,132	3,426,000	3,467,266	2,828,324
Teachers guides procured	236,816	485,195	549,150	593,480	637,811	673,533	686,297	118,123	254904

Source: EPD, Annual School Census (2004)

The greatest beneficiaries of UPE have been female children. Enrollment of girls soared to 3,632,838 in 2004, from only 1,420,883 in 1996; representing a 156% increase over the eight-year period of UPE implementation. Consequently, gender disparities in primary school enrollments have been almost wiped out because UPE has ensured a steady increase in the number of girls enrolling at school each year.

Figure 1: Trends in primary Pupil Enrollment (1996 – 2004)

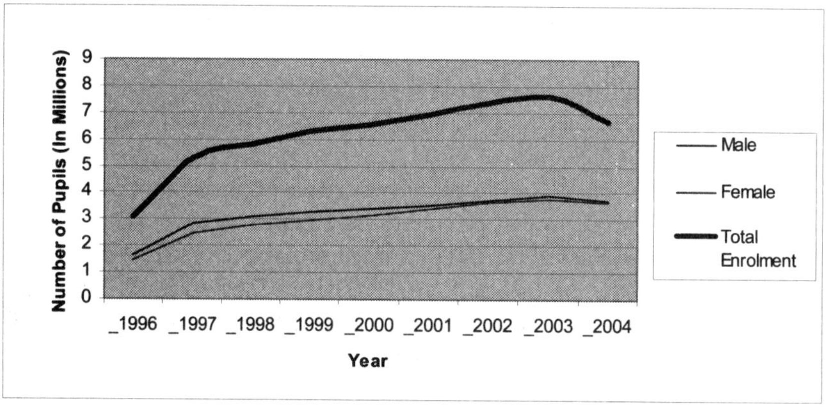

Source: EPD - Annual School Census, 2004.

In order to cater to rapid increases in pupil enrollments, while at the same time bringing education services closer to the children, the Government has tremendously expanded the school network. Prior to the implementation of UPE, there were only 8,531 Government-aided primary schools in the country. There is now over 13,000. This is in addition to about 2000 private primary schools in the country.

Figure 2: Growth in the Primary School Network (1996 – 2004)

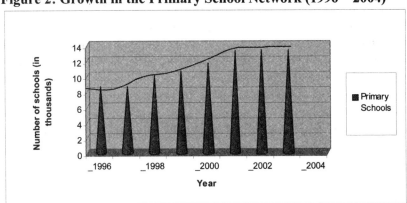

Source: EPD, Annual School Census (2004)

The stock of classrooms has increased by 205%. In 1996, there were only 25,676 classrooms in primary schools. However, because the School Facilities Grant (SFG) programme initiated by the Ministry of Education and Sports assists the most needy school communities to provide the basic primary school physical infrastructure, the number of classrooms has now increased to 78,403.

Figure 3: Trends in the Growth of Classroom Stock for Primary Schools

(1996 – 2004)

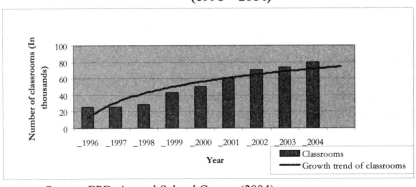

Source: EPD, Annual School Census (2004)

The rapid increases in school enrollments have also occasioned similar increases in the number of teachers. At the end of 1996, the primary school teaching force was only 81,600 teachers; the number now is 145,000 teachers -- out of which 85.1% are on Government payroll. In 1996, only about 40% of the teachers were on Government payroll.

Figure 4: Trends in the Recruitment of Primary School Teachers

(1996 – 2004)

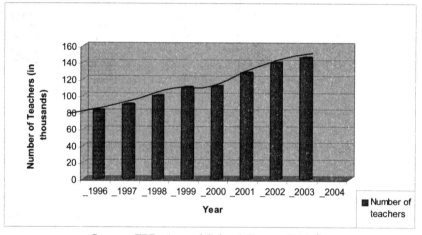

Source: EPD, Annual School Census (2004)

The pupil- teacher ratio is the proportion of pupils that would be attended to by a particular teacher in a school. The pupil-teacher ratios from year 2000 to 2004 have steadily and consistently been reduced at an annual rate of 7.4%. This has meant an improvement in terms of reduction in pressures on teachers and congestion of the learning environments of the pupils in schools. This is reflected in the declining curve in figure 5 below.

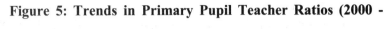

Figure 5: Trends in Primary Pupil Teacher Ratios (2000 - 2004)

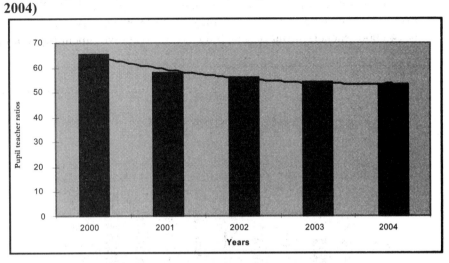

Source: EPD, Annual School Census (2004)

To ensure quality UPE, the Ministry of Education and Sports has spent a substantial proportion of its annual budget to increase the supply of instructional materials to schools. These include core textbooks; teacher guides; supplementary readers and non-text book materials. As a result of these efforts, the pupil textbook ratios have improved from 1:10 in 1996 to 1:3 in 2004. This is illustrated in the figure 6 below. The figure illustrates a decline in the number of textbooks procured in 2004 because procurements targeted the upper classes of P5 to P7 only.

Figure 6: Instructional Materials Procured (1996 – 2004)

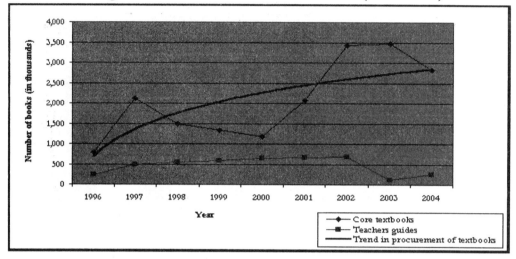

Source: Instructional Materials Unit, MoES

To confirm that the Ministry's efforts are bearing fruit, the percentage of pupils now reaching defined levels of competency in literacy and numeracy at P3 and P6 respectively has improved. In 2000, only 18% of pupils at P3 had reached defined levels of competency, by 2003 the figure is 34.3%. For children at P6, only 13% had reached the defined level of competency in literacy, four years later the proportion has improved to 20.5% With regard to competency in numeracy, while 39% of the children reached defined levels of numeracy in 2000, the proportion increased to 42.9% in 2003.

At the same time, the proportion of children successfully completing P7 has increased from 49.1% (2002) to 62% (2004). This surpassed the target of 60% that the Ministry had set for itself for 2004. While the completion rate of boys for P7 is still higher than that of girls (i.e. 72% for boys and 54% for girls), both these figures have exceeded the Ministry's 2004 targets by 1% for boys and 3% for girls.

Table 2:   Performance Indicators for the Primary Sub Sector

(2000-2004)

Indicator	2000	2001	2002	2003	2004
Pupil enrollment in all primary schools	6,559,013	6,900,916	7,354,153	7,633,314	7,354,749
Pupil enrollment in Government aided	5,351,099	5,917,216	6,575,827	6,835,525	6,695,998
Teachers on payroll	82,148	101,818	113,232	121,772	124,137
Number of classrooms	50,370	60,199	69,900	73,104	79,132
Pupil-teacher ratio	65	58	56	56	54
Pupil-classroom ratio	106	98	94	94	85
Enrollment growth rate	-	11%	11%	4%	-2%
Pupil textbook ratio	6:1	4:11	3:1	3:1	3:1
Percentage of pupils reaching defined level of competency in literacy at (a) P3 (b) P6	18% 13%	N/A	N/A	34.3% 20.5%	N/A
Percentage of pupils reaching defined level of competency in numeracy at (a) P3 (b) P6	39% 41%	N/A	N/A	42.9% 20.5%	N/A
Completion rate-P7 (a) Boys (b) Girls		62.9% 71.1% 54.9%	49.1% 58.8% 41.0%	56% 66% 47%	62% 72% 54%

Source: Education Planning Department, Annual School Census 2004

Progress Towards Gender Parity in Education

By 2004, enrollment in formal primary schools in Uganda stood at 3,872,589 boys and 3,760,725 girls. Enrollment in non-formal programmes had 20,567 boys and 27,248 girls in primary education. Among children who enroll in P1, 68.8% of girls, as opposed to 66.3% of boys, reach P4. Of those, 20.9% girls compared to 24.1 boys go on to P7. Among children who repeat classes 14.2% are boys as opposed to 13.5% girls. On the whole, boys tend to repeat more, but girls mostly drop out altogether.

Gender disparities in education are hence mostly caused by the high dropout rates of girls in upper primary school characterized by low retention, repetition, dropout and non-completion. Thus, while Countrywide enrollment figures for girls are fairly good in P1 and P2 (48% girls; 52% boys), from P4 onwards there is a widening of the gender gap. The completion rate for girls in 2003 was 65% while that of boys was 71%.

Figure 7 indicates the ratio of girls to boys in the primary education sub-sector: It can be seen that the gender gap has been narrowing since 2000 and is tending to 1:1.

Figure 7: Ratios of Girls to Boys (Primary)

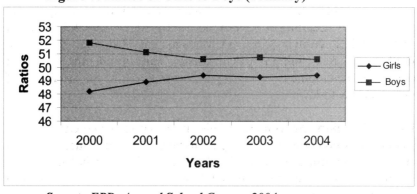

Source: EPD, Annual School Census, 2004

In the secondary sub-sector, there have been improvements in the participation of girls. Figure 8 indicates that in 2000, the ratio of girls to boys stood at 44.1% to 55.9%. This ratio improved from 45.0% to 55.0% in the year 2004.

84

Figure 9: Ratios of Girls to Boys (Secondary)

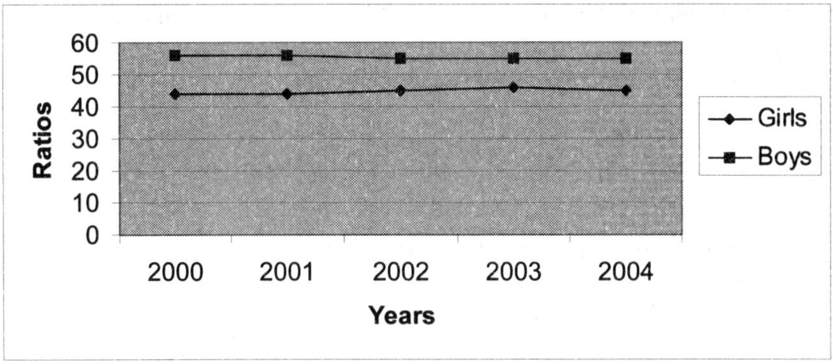

Source: EPD, Annual School Census, 2004

Key Initiatives in Enhancing Basic Education for Girls

In an effort to accelerate girls' full and equal participation and retention in primary schools, the Government of Uganda has embarked on a number of programmes which are currently being implemented under the Education Sector Investment Plan (ESIP). These include among others; the Girls' Education Movement (GEM), the National Strategy for Girls Education in Uganda, the Child Friendly Basic Education and Learning Programme (2001-2005), Breakthrough to Literacy (BTL), Growing Up and Management of Sexual Maturation (GUSM), the Sara initiative, and Basic Education Child Care and Adolescent Development (BECCAD). A review of the key elements of these programs follows.

Girls' Education Movement: This is a child centered, girl-led, grassroots movement to empower girls to take action on issues central to furthering their education. In each school, the GEM club is led by girls, with boys as strategic allies and adult women and men advisors who provide the wisdom of age. The local GEM clubs are started by students who have attended a GEM facilitator training. Over 100 young people have been trained at GEM trainings and GEM clubs are being started in schools throughout the districts.

The key activities of GEM include; conducting school and community mapping exercises that identify out-of-school youth in the community; identifying barriers to school attendance for girls and developing strategies to overcome these barriers; engaging in community awareness efforts designed to sensitise parents and community leaders about the value of girls' education and the issues girls face; developing partnerships with boys and schools leaders to more effectively address the issues identified; and designing and conducting peer education efforts aimed at issues of safety, security, and life skills training on health and sexuality issues.

National Strategy for Girls Education: This has been formulated as a partnership with other stakeholders and harmonizes their roles and activities in educating female children. It outlines key barriers to girls' education in Uganda and provides various strategies to address them.

Early Childhood Development: This programme aims at training local women in health and child development strategies that enhance the early development of the child. It has the effect of freeing girls from the responsibility of caring for younger siblings in order that they may attend school and it supports establishing early positive habits for girls education.

Child Friendly Basic Education and Learning Programme: This program emphasizes a comprehensive approach to issues of quality education, equitable participation attainments, retention and addressing the challenges of education for the excluded, including female children.

Breakthrough To Literacy: This is a teaching methodology based in the local language designed to teach children life skills and to read and write in their mother tongues. This is an interactive, participatory methodology that is child-centered and gender responsive supporting girls' retention.

The Sara Initiative: The Sara initiative is a programme which aims at raising the awareness of the general public to the importance of supporting girls' education, building their self esteem and raising their life aspiration.

Basic Education Child Care and Adolescent Development: This program focuses on the rights of children and promotes awareness about girls' education at the basic level, paying special attention to increasing female enrollments.

All these interventions are aimed at lowering social-cultural barriers to girls' attendance and retention in primary education. However, despite the assistance by international and local agencies, and the well acclaimed political goodwill and commitment, which has recently improved Uganda's achievements in advancing female enrollment in primary education, Uganda still falls short in achievement of girls' universal primary education completion.

Main Challenges of Universal Primary Education in Uganda

The introduction of Universal Primary Education in 1997 and its implementation have been a great success. It has led to an enrollment increase from about 3 million in 1996, to over 7.3 million in 2004. The 1997 P.1 entrants completed the primary seven cycle in 2003 and this required a response from Government on how to accommodate this big bulge of potential UPE graduates into post primary education.

While the high gross enrollment ratio in primary schooling signals that most and probably all, students attend primary school at some stage, completion rates have remained low. There are high rates of attrition between each grade, so that only a small percentage of those who enter actually complete the full cycle. The progress of the 2.16 million student cohort that enrolled in P1 in 1997 is as follows: only 1.3 million proceeded to P2; 1.1 million to P3; 0.96 million to P4; 0.83 million to P5; 0.7 million to P6; and only 0.48 million survived to make it to P7 in 2003. The big drop is attributed to three factors: most children who started P1 were under-age, repetition of different levels and drop-out rates.

Not only are the rates of drop out before grade 5 economically and educationally wasteful, but those who drop-out are likely to become functionally illiterate adults. The main challenges facing the UPE program therefore centre around the following factors which characterize Uganda:

(i)   The country has one of the highest population growth rates in the world (3.4%). For this reason, Uganda has to work hard to sustain basic services such as UPE. These numbers have implications for resource availability and budget allocations among the sub-sectors.

(ii)   HIV/AIDS is a serious challenge, causing many teachers to suffer from poor health, leading to frequent absenteeism. Thousands of HIV/AIDS orphans are in school, some are HIV positive and others take care of their sick family members. HIV/AIDS also contributes to rising drop out rates, absenteeism, repetition and poor academic performance and overall poor quality education. In order to solve this problem, in 2002 the Presidential Initiative on AIDS Strategy for Communication to Youths (PIASCY) was launched to sensitise children and the youth on HIV/AIDS. PIASCY assemblies are conducted in every school bi-monthly.

(iii)   Operating with fixed budgets is a challenge. In order to continue and improve on UPE, Government will have to retain, or even increase, the national and education budgets so as to improve access and quality. There are however, other competing demands on the budget. In addition, districts often are unable to allocate significant proportions of their local revenue to supplement the capitation grants provided under UPE

(iv)   Providing education in areas disturbed by conflict is a serious challenge to basic education. An estimated one and a half, to two million pupils were affected by conflict during 2003 in the north, north-east and parts of western Uganda.

(v)   Infrastructure and material/equipment is still lacking. Although Government has done a commendable job in infrastructure development, the construction of these facilities is not yet at pace with the rate of increases in school enrollments. Given the financial and other investments involved, this remains a major challenge.

(vi)   There is general lack of coordination between the centre and local governments, and in some cases a lack of clarity of roles. Synchronizing central and local government planning and programme management is still a serious challenge. However, coordinating mechanisms are being introduced to address this problem.

(vii)   Widening the participation of local leaders and communities must be continued. The greatest challenge the UPE programme has been facing with regard to sustainability is a limited sense of ownership and sense of responsibility among local communities. In order to solve this problem, the Government of Uganda has developed a multi-media strategy campaign to mobilize the stakeholders to participate and contribute in the implementation of UPE.

(viii)   Regular supervision, monitoring and evaluation of programmes must be retained. There has been inadequate monitoring and supervision of this important programme. The linkage between school inspection and the Education Standards Agency needs to be streamlined.   In order to solve this problem, grants are deducted for this activity to enhance supervision by inspectors.

The Plan to Introduce Universal Secondary Education

In anticipation of the UPE "batch" completing Primary 7 in 2003, the Ministry of Education and Sports (MOES) developed policies on Post-Primary Education and Training (PPET), and is planning to induce universal secondary education (USE). The challenge is not only to increase the proportion of pupils completing P7 but also to increase the number of those pupils who go on to further education and training after P7. Only about 50% of the pupils who left P7 in 2003 made the transition to post primary education training.

Government has already embarked on the process of universalizing secondary education. Various strategies and policies have been put in place in a bid to enhance access to post primary education. These include subsidizing secondary education through capitation grants to Government secondary schools. Each student is paid Shs.61 Per day, which amounts to 18,000 per term, per student. A total of 65 billion Shilling is spent every financial year on this capitation grant for secondary education.

A total of 47,700 students are benefiting from a bursary scheme that contributes for schools fees for children whose parents live in internally displaced peoples (IDP) camps in war ravaged areas. A total of 3bn Shs was available in the recent Mid-Term Budget Framework (MTBF) for this purpose although the required amount is 6bnShs at a unit contribution rate of 47,700 per student, per term.

Three years ago, Government introduced the secondary education bursary scheme for needy but bright students attending secondary education. Two students from all sub-counties are nominated every year for this program. To date, close to 5,500 students are benefiting from this bursary scheme at a cost of 270,000 per year per student. This past financial year, 1.6bn Shs has been provided in the Medium Term Budget framework.

Other initiatives include grants aiding community schools and, to date, 196 community schools have been grant-aided since 2001 to bring the total number of both public and government-aided secondary schools close to 840. In line with the President's "Manifesto" 20 secondary schools have been constructed since 2001 in a bid to increase the number of sub-counties with a secondary school. For the many pupils for whom vocational training is more appropriate, 16 community polytechnics have been set up and are operating; and 14 more are under construction.

Secondary Education Sub-Sector: In 2000, enrollments in secondary education stood at 518,931 students and these increased to 721,212 in 2004 with 78% attending private secondary schools. Consequently, over this four-year period, MoES has registered 40% increase in access to secondary education.

Figure 9: Trends in Total Enrollment in Secondary Schools (1996 - 2004)

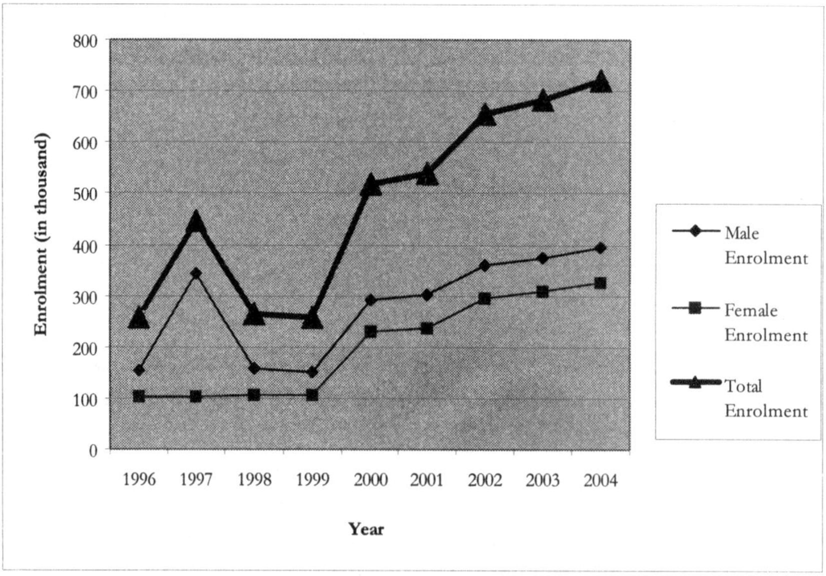

Source: EPD, Annual School Census, 2004

Furthermore, the proportion of students attending secondary school compared to the number of 13 – 18 year olds in the entire population has increased from 13% in 2000 to 21% in 2004, with an 8% increase for boys and a 7% increase for girls over the four year period.

Figure 10: Trends in Gross Enrollment Ratio in Secondary Education (2000 – 2004)

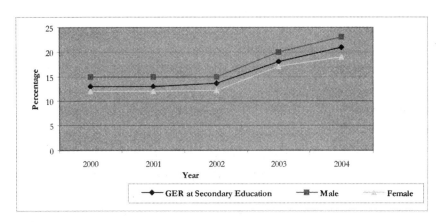

However, on the negative side, the gender gap in secondary education still persists. The gender gap is likely to be reduced over time since the sector has provided for several gender related educational initiatives and the transition rate to Senior 1 for girls is higher than that of their male counterparts. In 2003, transition rates for boys stood at 57% and that of girls at 63%. In 2004, transition rate had increased to 61% for boys and 68% for girls. However, the transition rate for boys to Senior 5 is generally higher than that of girls (i.e. 43% for boys and 33% for girls in 2004).

Table 3: Trends in Transition Rate to S1 and S5 (2000-2004)

Transition Rate	2000	2001	2002	2003	2004
S1	65%	61%	69%	59%	64%
i) Boys	61%	56%	65%	57%	61%
ii) Girls	70%	66%	74%	63%	68%
S5	43%	31%	41%	42%	39%
i) Boys	42%	34%	43%	45%	43%
ii) Girls	43%	28%	49%	39%	33%

Despite the sharp decline in 2003, there is an evident increase in the Senior Four completion rate between 2000 and 2004. This is reflected in the increasing trend line. Also, there are still more male completers of senior four than females.

Figure 11: Trends in Completion Rate of Senior Four (2000 to 2004)

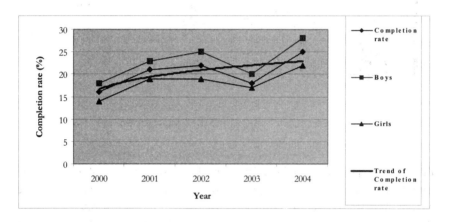

Business, Technical, Vocational Educational Training: Likewise in Business, Technical, Vocational Educational Training (BTVET), total enrollment has steadily grown from 14,077 students in 2000, to 26,313 students in 2003, representing an 86.9% increase in total enrollment over a four-year period. The government has also registered success in narrowing the gender enrollment gap in BTVET institutions - with an increase in female enrollment share from 10.4% in 2000, to 30.6% in 2003.

Figure 12: Enrollment Growth Patterns in BTVET Institutions

(2000 to 2004)

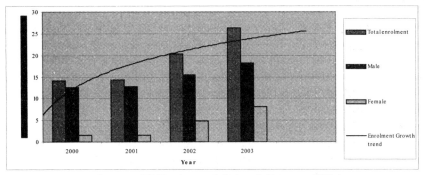

Source: EPD, Annual School Census, 2004

Female Participation in Post-Primary Education: A number of factors have affected female participation in post primary education. The introduction or modification of post primary education programmes have in most cases had positive outcomes for the enrollment of female students as the description in the paragraphs below suggest.

The restructuring of specialized health training institutions helped to push female enrollment to 4,756 out of the total 5,170. In addition, minimum entry requirements for nursing courses were revised with positive results for enrollment of female students.

The introduction of more courses in the BTVET institutions (such as home economics in Community Polytechnics (CPs), and painting and decoration in Technical Institutes) that are popular with females has helped increase access. In addition, new diploma courses in industrial ceramics & refrigeration and air conditioning at UTC Bushenyi and Nakawa Vocational Training Institutes have offered further access for girls.

The introduction of Gender Focal Point Officers in GEM, and the management of sexual maturation, has enhanced the tutors' and student teachers' ability to handle gender related issues across the curriculum. Altogether, twenty - two Outreach deputy principals, twenty-

93

two Pre-service deputy principals and some PTC principals and heads of programmes have benefited from the training on the management of sexual maturation.

Proposal to Introduce Universal Secondary Education: One of the greatest achievements of UPE in Uganda has also turned out to be one of the Country's greatest social challenges. This is the question of what to do for the very large number of children who have graduated from the primary school system and who qualify for admission to the secondary school system but whose parents or guardians cannot economically support them at this level. Consequently, Government came up with the decision to introduce Universal Secondary Education (USE) to address this situation.

This policy, which is due to be implemented by the year 2007, has as many opponents as it has supporters. Each side of the debate has put forward equally strong reasons for or against the proposal. Those against USE argue that since the resources available were not adequate to support UPE efficiently, expansion should be avoided and steps should be taken to strengthen the implementation of the UPE policy instead. Those supporting USE, on the other hand, argue that the students who have graduated from UPE should be given the opportunity to continue and that this step should inspire those who are still in the UPE System, together with their parents and guardians.

Regardless of the outcome of this debate, Government is determined to implement USE by adjusting priorities in other areas of development. To that end, steps are underway to increase the number of teachers and other complementary resources to ensure that the policy is implemented on schedule by the close of 2007. There will be many lessons to be learnt about public administration from this experiment. Indeed, the Office of the Prime Minister has a plan to document the critical experiences of these programmes and to analyze their implications for enhancement of Government capacity to implement its development programmes.

Conclusion and a Look to the Future

The experiences of implementing UPE in Uganda, as described in this paper should be humbling for all leaders of resource poor countries that are struggling to eradicate poverty. The overall resources needed to effectively implement UPE and effectively address the needs of the students who graduate from the system are astronomical in size. In addition, the task of putting in place the social, political and economic condition required to implement this and other Millennium Development Goals is daunting.

In brief, the following are sorbering observations from the UPE implementation experience. UPE is a great need but Uganda has other competing urgent needs. To continue and improve, UPE will have to retain and even increase its share of the national and education budgets. Only about 50% of the required infrastructure is now in place. Maintaining its share of the education budget will probably be UPE's biggest challenge. There is need to spend more on post-primary education as the "UPE bulge" moves up. Primary education's portion of Education budget may stabilize at about 60%, down from the current 67%.

Teacher attrition rate create logistical and financial problems. About seven per cent of primary teachers quit teaching every year. Some leave due to sickness. Others go to teach in private schools or look for jobs outside teaching. Many teachers would rather leave teaching than work in hard–to-reach areas. Teachers in such areas receive an additional 20% incentive allowance on top of their salary. The impact of this incentive has yet to be evaluated. However, hard-to-reach areas continue to be underserved.

The Government has decentralized education services management to the districts. The districts now have the power to make reasonable decisions and manage funds remitted to them from the central government. However, there is need for further capacity building to handle tendering mechanisms, accountability of funds, and education management information systems. A study conducted to track the flow of, and accountability for, UPE funds from the central government to schools providing UPE revealed that there are tremendous problems of financial management and administration that call for further capacity building for local governments.

95

The first phase of UPE has been challenging. There was tremendous pressure on the educational infrastructure. However, the Government rapidly developed systems to cope with the influx. By the year 2004, many of the indicators of quality such as the pupil-teacher ratio and pupil-textbook ratio were better than before UPE. This was largely due to Government's financial commitments, which had been consistent.

One major conclusion from the Uganda UPE implementation experience is that all Millennium Development Goals need further re-examination to reveal their realistic implementation requirements. In anticipation of the findings of that exercise, the rich nations of the world must be prepared to support the efforts of developing countries in achieving these very noble development goals. The requirements for the implementation of the Millennium Development Goals are extensive and cannot be wished away by the development community.

There are several areas in which more support for poor countries is urgently required if the Millennium Development Goals (MDGs) are to be achieved on schedule. First, there is a further need for capacity building. Too few qualified technical personnel are available in all relevant areas. This is especially the case where decentralization of Government has been adopted. There are not enough qualified people at the local government level and a relatively few qualified people are available at the centre.

Second, the implementation of virtually all MDGs calls for more infrastructure in the form of buildings, equipment, information and communication technology. Third, human resource development touches on a very wide range of development programmes. More human resources of all kinds are required. The intervention of rich nations in these areas is urgently required. This underlines the need referred to earlier for further examination of MDGs to reveal more specifically the areas in which further assistance is needed.

Migration and the Contemporary World: Addressing Key Issues and Challenges on a Global Level

By

Patricia Sto. Thomas[*]

In the last century, the world as we know it has been heavily transformed by the process of globalization. Rapid advancements in technology have facilitated the quick and effortless exchange of both information and goods and services in an increasingly interlinked global community. Our once vast and immense world of seven continents and 193 countries has now been compressed into an accessible international village where transference is not limited to products and ideas. In recent history, people have also begun to move freely and easily in this global environment -- unrestricted by limits of time, boundaries and distance.

With the extensive globalization of labor markets, migration motivated by employment considerations must be thoroughly analyzed. Existing labor migration trends and procedures must be systematically evaluated and assessed, and a comprehensive global initiative is needed to streamline and improve current labor-related migration policies and systems across the world. This paper describes the architecture of a labor migration policy which will meet considerations for orderly management, as well as protect migrant rights and welfare. The Philippine overseas employment system, which has been under implementation for over three decades, is offered as a case study. As such, it is an example of the kind of citizen oriented public policy which countries in transition must adopt in order to enhance their possibility of achieving the Millennium Development Goals.

Managing Migration; Managing Tensions

The large-scale impacts of globalization brings with it the inextricably attached issue of human migration. In this modern world, where the global economy is rapidly expanding, there has been a marked

---

[*] Secretary for Labor and Employment, Philippines and former member of the Committee of Experts on Public Administration of the United Nations.

increase in the movements of people seeking better opportunities and living conditions overseas. No country has been untouched by international migration. If the migrants of the world were to be accommodated in one territory, it would approximate Brazil, the fifth most populous nation on earth.

More significantly, the numbers will continue to grow. Estimates indicate that the number of migrants in the world doubled in the past 25 years, and the next doubling is expected within an even shorter period. Human mobility is accelerating, helped by advances in transportation and communications, but also propelled by socio-economic and political realities – both within and across nations. Migration is likely to be a central issue of the 21st century and one that will continue to generate significant debate and discussion.

According to the UNDP, the proportion of the world's population living in poverty has fallen faster in the past 50 years than in the previous 500 years. Nonetheless, there is still a substantial gap between living standards in richer and poorer parts of the globe. In 1975, the per capita GDP in high-income countries was 41 times greater than that in low-income countries and eight times greater than that in middle-income countries. Today, high-income countries have per capita GDPs that are 66 times those of low-income countries and 14 times those of middle-income countries.

These statistics explain why migration is mainly a South-North movement and why high-income countries, which have less than 20% of the global labor force, now host over 60% of the world's migrants. Migrants in high-income countries earn incomes 20 or 30 times higher than they would normally earn in their respective home countries. While the cost of living is usually much higher in countries of destination, most migrants have the potential to earn enough to support themselves and send remittances to their families back home.

Despite market-oriented reforms in developing countries, labor surpluses still tend to push workers in search of overseas work opportunities. At destination countries, the demand for migrant workers is strong. In industrialized states, the increasing competitiveness of the global economy has placed new pressures on firms to minimize costs and maximize the use of cheap and flexible labor --- the kind of jobs which migrants are willing to provide.

World Bank indicators show that the global labor force will rise from 3 to 3.4 billion in the period of 2001 to 2010, an average increase of 40 million per year. Thirty-eight million of that annual growth is expected to come from developing countries, the remainder from high-income countries. With this trend, about 86% of the world's labor force will come from developing countries. The numbers are expected to fill in the human resource gaps in industrialized countries, particularly in providing care for aging persons and in supporting pension systems.

Migration is an age-old, continuing and inevitable phenomenon. It is also a multi-pronged issue which has significantly affected various levels of human existence. Throughout the course of time, the widely-encompassing issue of international migration has created dramatic tensions all across the world. It has spawned bitter social conflicts, political violence, cultural and religious upheavals, economic hostilities, security threats and a host of other tensions among peoples and nations.

It is critically necessary that these issues be properly addressed by the international community. Migration must be managed universally in order to minimize the tensions generated by different diasporic processes. Labor migration -- which is contract-based, temporary and circular -- provides one model which the present global environment can use.

The Global Commission on International Migration (GCIM), a consultative body composed of 19 Commissioners, formed upon the encouragement of UN Secretary General Kofi Annan, figures prominently in this effort. In fulfillment of its mandate, the GCIM endeavored to present a coherent, comprehensive and global response to the migration phenomenon. After a series of consultative meetings held in different parts of the world, the Commission outlined a normative framework for the formulation of consistent international migration policies. One result of these consultations has been six salient points which have been called the GCIM's Principles for Action, a framework which, in the future, could be used as a guide by governments in drafting coherent and effective policies for managing migration.

In view of this background, we shall employ the GCIM's Principles for Action as a benchmark and point of reference in assessing and analyzing current migration policies and standards, with regard to how the Philippines acts in accordance with the GCIM's established working framework in the context of contemporary labor migration.

The Global Commission on International Migration

In the global arena, the issue of international migration has inevitably grown in scale, speed, scope and complexity. This multidimensional subject has already started to occupy the forefront of the global agenda as governments, multilateral organizations, civil society and other worldwide stakeholders have felt the pressing need to address the impacts and relevance of migration in modern times.

It was against this backdrop that the Global Commission on International Migration (GCIM) was born. Launched by a number of governments (including the Philippines) on December 9, 2003, and encouraged by UN Secretary General Kofi Annan, the GCIM sought to provide a framework for the formulation of a coherent, comprehensive and global response to the issue of international migration. It received support from the governments of Sweden, Switzerland, the Netherlands, the United Kingdom, Norway, Australia and Germany, as well as the MacArthur Foundation, the Ford Foundation and the World Bank.

An independent body consisting of 19 members of various nationalities with extensive international experience and expertise on migration, the GCIM was specifically requested to:

a) promote a comprehensive debate among states and other actors with respect to migration;
b) analyze gaps in current policy approaches to migration;
c) examine inter-linkages between migration and other global issues and;
d) present appropriate recommendations to the UN Secretary General, government and other stakeholders.

After having conducted a series of five fruitful consultative hearings in the Philippines, Egypt, Hungary, South Africa and Mexico over an eighteen-month period, the GCIM presented their findings contained in the report, *Migration in an Interconnected World: New directions for action.*

The recommendations resulting from this effort were subsequently condensed into six concise action points dealing with a wide array of migration-related themes including labor migration, irregular migration, the reinforcement of migration's economic and developmental impacts, social integration, migrants' rights and the enhancement of the governance of international migration. Drafted by the GCIM to primarily serve as an international normative framework for migration management, these six core principles can now be employed as a guide by governments for the formulation of coherent, comprehensive and effective migration policies.

Principles for Action[*]

I.   Migration out of choice: Migration and the global economy: Women, men and children should be able to realize their potential, meet their needs, exercise their human rights and fulfill their aspirations in their country of origin, and hence migrate out of choice, rather than necessity. Those women and men who migrate and enter the global labor market should be able to do so in a safe and authorized manner, and because they and their skills are valued and needed by the states and societies that receive them.

II.   Reinforcing economic and developmental impact: The role that migrants play in promoting development and poverty reduction in countries of origin, as well as the contribution they make towards the prosperity of destination countries, should be recognized and reinforced. International migration should become an integral part of national, regional and global strategies for economic growth, in both the developing and developed world.

III. Addressing irregular migration: States, exercising their sovereign right to determine who enters and remains on their territory, should fulfill their responsibility and obligation to protect the rights of migrants and to re-admit those citizens who wish, or are obliged, to return to their country of origin. In stemming irregular migration, states should actively cooperate with one another, ensuring that their efforts do not jeopardize human rights, including the rights of refugees to seek asylum. Governments should consult with employers, trade unions and civil society on this issue.

---

[*] The six principles that follow are reprinted in full from *Migration in an Interconnected World: New directions for action* (Report of the Global Commission on International Migration)

IV.   Strengthening social cohesion through integration: Migrants, and citizens of destination countries, should respect their legal obligations and benefit from a mutual process of adaptation and integration that accommodates cultural diversity and fosters social cohesion. The integration process should be actively supported by local and national authorities, employers and members of civil society, and should be based on a commitment to non-discrimination and gender equity. It should also be informed by an objective public, political and media discourse on international migration.

V.   Protecting the rights of migrants: The legal and normative framework affecting international migrants should be strengthened, implemented more effectively and applied in a non-discriminatory manner, in order to protect the human rights and labor standards that should be enjoyed by all migrant women and men. Respecting the provisions of this legal and normative framework, states and other stakeholders must address migration issues in a more consistent and coherent manner.

VI.   Enhancing governance: Coherence, capacity and cooperation: The governance of international migration should be enhanced by improved coherence and strengthened capacity at the national level; greater consultation and cooperation between states at the regional level; and more effective dialogue and cooperation among governments and between international organizations at the global level. Such efforts must be based on a better appreciation of the close linkages that exist between international migration and development and other key policy issues, including trade, aid, state security, human security and human rights.

Overseas Employment:
Philippine Migration to Globalized Labor Markets

Overseas employment has become a central component and cornerstone of the Philippine economy. While Filipinos are generally

102

mobile, a function of the archipelagic nature of Philippine territory, organized movements may actually be traced to the mid-70s. The Middle East economies started massive development efforts as a result of the increased oil revenues and turned to the Philippines, among other countries, for needed human resources.

In an effort to address rising unemployment and balance-of-payments problems, the Philippine government initiated an Overseas Employment Program in 1974 in order to facilitate the placement of Filipino workers abroad. Initially, the government directly managed the deployment of workers with employers overseas, but soon devolved the function to private recruitment agencies and assumed a more limited oversight role.

Leaving for overseas jobs has since become an embedded feature of Philippine culture. In the majority of Filipino households, at least one relative has been, or is currently, employed abroad. Overseas Filipino Workers (OFWs) are ubiquitously scattered throughout the world, taking on a myriad of blue-collar and white-collar positions. It is an indisputable fact that in virtually every country in the world there is a Filipino national working as a nurse, domestic helper, engineer, entertainer, cook, teacher, welder, driver, programmer, and possibly every other job imaginable. With their reputation for resilience, dependability and a good work ethic, coupled with a caring nature and facility in the English language, members of the Filipino workforce remain highly marketable and sought after by employers worldwide.

Mass labor migration in Philippine society has always been motivated mainly by financial considerations. With the population explosion came increased levels of poverty incidence and unemployment in the country, and thus international labor markets had to be explored by the government and the members of the Filipino workforce as a catch basin for domestic unemployment.

Starting with an average of 50,000 in the 70s, the number of Filipino workers deployed for overseas jobs increased to an annual average of 390,000 in the 80s and 660,000 in the 90s. In 2004, deployment reached a high of 933,588. In the first semester of 2005, global deployment rose by almost 10 percent reaching 541,201; an increase from 493,947 for the same period in 2004. This means that about 2900 Filipinos leave daily to work overseas. Estimates of Filipinos overseas in 2005 reveal more than 8 million individuals in over 194 countries.

Top Ten Destinations of Overseas Filipino Workers (OFWs)	
Rank/Country	2001 - 2004
1. K. of Saudi Arabia (KSA)	188,107
2. Hong Kong	87,254
3. United Arab Emirates (UAE)	68,386
4. Japan	74,480
5. Taiwan	45,059
6. Kuwait	36,591
7. Qatar	21,360
8. Singapore	22,198
9. Italy	23,329
10. United Kingdom	18,347

Source: Philippine Overseas Employment Administration

Remittances of the Filipino Migrant Workers

Equally as important as the impact on unemployment is the significant contribution that the Filipino migrant workers are making to the Country's economy through their inward remittances. The increasing volume of deployment, and the increasing number of skilled workers with higher compensation, boosted the remittances sent home which reached US$ 1.8 billion in 1990 and hit an all time high of US$ 8.5 billion in 2004. With the growth of 4.9 percent in Net Factor Income from Abroad (NFIA) or remittances, coming mostly from an increase in compensation income of OFWs, the Philippine Gross National Product (GNP) grew by 6.1 percent, up from 5.6 percent in the previous year. During the crisis years, GNP managed to register a positive growth, though minimal, primarily because of the remittances of overseas workers.

These remittances have fuelled local investments in real estate (as more overseas workers are able to invest in their own house and lot) and a host of small and medium enterprises (neighborhood convenience stores or "sari-sari stores", beauty parlors, welding shops, computer or video rental shops, jeepneys or tricycles, soap and other personal care products and manufacturing, among others). The remittances have greatly improved the standard of living of the migrant workers and their families - many are able to build decent houses in their provinces or localities, their children are able to go to better schools, families are able to acquire household appliances and many are able to have access to better medical and health facilities.

The Philippine Overseas Employment System as a Global Model

In the field of labor migration, the outdated paradigm of permanent migrant settlement has since evolved into the more modern and dynamic model of temporary circular migration. In response to this trend, concerted national efforts have been exerted to manage migration and ensure that internal and external tensions are mitigated. The Philippine overseas employment system may perhaps be best denominated as the management of contract migration. As a result of the great worldwide demand for Filipino labor, the system for managing migration has evolved to the highly regulated system that it is today. The components of this system are: regulation, protection and reintegration.

Among the 10 labor-sending nations of the Asian continent, the Philippines boasts of a structured and regulated system of contract migration that covers the entire employment process from pre-employment, onsite employment, to post employment or reintegration upon the migrant worker's return to the country. The supervision by government was perfected on the intervening three decades of continuous migratory flows and over the same time, changes in the regulatory structure emerged. Emerging origin countries look to the Philippine model for emulation as a government-supervised migration architecture.

Regulation: for migration in the Philippines involves of a number of official interventions. There is the licensing system for recruitment agents that prescribes standards for participation and continuance in the business. The Philippine Overseas Employment Administration (POEA), an attached agency of the Department of Labor and Employment, exercises supervision over private sector participation in the overseas employment program through an organized system of licensing and registration which includes:

- issuance of licenses to business entities engaged in recruitment of workers for overseas employment;

- a policy of registration of foreign employers who are permitted to employ the services of Philippine contractual labor;
- issuance of defined rules and procedures for foreign employment, with corresponding incentives and penalties;
- enforcement of contractual and wage standards;
- exit controls at major ports, where departing migrants are required to submit proof of compliance to the foregoing employment protocols; and
- maintenance of a database of all workers processed through the system.

The POEA sets the standards for recruitment fees, wages and working conditions, repatriation of workers and the posting of bonds to answer for possible workers' claims and penalties for recruitment violations. Violations of these standards become ground for license cancellation. The absence of a license, on the other hand, is a ground for charges of illegal recruitment. Illegal recruitment is a non-bailable offense when it affects three or more people. A task force against illegal recruitment operates to prevent innocent or ignorant applicants from being fleeced of their money.

Part of the system is the registration and accreditation of foreign employers by the POEA to ensure the existence of the principal and/or projects and its manpower requirements. Employers with records of violation of employment contracts, abuse or exploitation of their workers are blacklisted. Employment contracts of workers selected by a licensed agent need to be processed and approved by the POEA, copies of which are put on file together with other details of the workers' overseas employment history. The workers also are enrolled for health and life insurance so that their welfare concerns are properly addressed.

Applicants for overseas employment are required to submit authenticated certificates from one of the networks of trade testing centers attesting to their acquired skills and medical certificates from accredited hospitals and medical clinics attesting to their physical fitness for the jobs. Once they pass the selection process and obtain approval to work abroad, they are required to attend a Pre-Departure Orientation Seminar (PDOS) to enable them to fully understand the migration procedures, their rights and obligations under their employment contracts, the cultural norms of their country of destination and to provide other vital information that will prepare them in adapting to their overseas jobs.

Prior to entering this process, Pre-Employment Orientation Seminars (PEOS) are conducted to apprise would-be applicants about the risks and possible problems of overseas employment. These orientations are country-specific and serve as a first screen for people who might wish to go and work abroad. The PEOS also include warnings against illegal-recruitment racketeers and values orientation for prospective OFWs. Initially conducted by POEA, the conduct of PEOS has now been devolved to the local government units for better reach down to the grassroots level.

Another part of the pre-departure services is the Labor Assistance Center (LAC), which acts as an extension of the POEA at the airport to assist workers during the final checking of their documents before they proceed to Immigration. The LAC is electronically linked with the POEA to facilitate access to a common database and issuance of travel clearance The LAC also acts as *watch posts* in airports, an extra protection to ensure non-trafficking of workers.

Information on the overseas employment policies of the government, laws and rules on overseas employment, the latest guidelines released by POEA, job vacancies and list of licensed recruitment agencies can be accessed through the POEA website. Complementing the website is the POEA Assistance Center which provides the above information and assistance to POEA clients and the general public through a 24-hour hotline numbers.

Protection: Employed beyond territorial boundaries of the sending country, contract migrants are prone to be subjected to sub-standard terms and conditions of employment. As the POEA exercises oversight over recruitment agencies within the Philippines, the same agencies are required to insure full compliance to overseas employment standards by the foreign employers. There is a *joint and solidary liability* component in the agency licensing rules where the Philippine agent is held co-liable for the actions of the foreign employer it represents. This agency liability pertains to the enforcement of the terms and conditions of the employment contract, and to ensure humane treatment of the migrant at worksites abroad.

On-site, a world-wide corps of labor and welfare attaches acts as the operating arm of the Department of Labor and Employment to provide protection and assistance to Filipino migrant workers. There are about 200 labor and welfare officers in missions/consulates or embassies in over 35 countries attending to Filipino migrant workers at any point in time. These officers are either lawyers, doctors, or social welfare officers. They attend to verification of employment contracts, as well as, cases of contract violations, maltreatment and abuse, and even repatriation of sick persons or the remains of workers when the occasion so requires.

The Migrant Workers and Overseas Act of 1995 has concretized the Philippine Government's commitment to protect the rights and promote the welfare of migrant workers, their families and other overseas Filipinos in distress. The Office of Legal Assistance for Migrant Workers Affairs was established within the Department of Foreign Affairs responsible for the provision and overall coordination of all legal assistance services to migrant workers and overseas Filipinos in distress. The Office manages the Legal Assistance Fund, which was set up to pay for legal services of foreign lawyers, court fees and charges and other litigation expenses.

An Emergency Repatriation Fund was also established for the repatriation of workers in cases of war, epidemic, disaster, calamities and other similar events, and in cases of repatriation of workers where the foreign principal or recruitment agency cannot be identified. However, normally the repatriation of migrant workers is the primary responsibility of the foreign principal and/or recruitment agency.

Filipino Workers Resource Centers are established within the Philippine Embassy premises in countries where there is a large concentration of Filipino migrant workers to serve as a 24-hour information and assistance center. The Centers provide counseling, legal and welfare services, as well as programs to promote social integration, settlement and community networking. They also serve as home and shelter for Filipino migrant workers in distress and also as a training venue to improve and upgrade the skills of workers through short-term courses on computer usage, food preparation, bar tending, sewing and even financial planning. Counseling on alternative occupations or livelihood are also conducted, particularly for returning Filipino migrant workers.

Welfare Programs: Unique in the Philippine context, there is a welfare office, the Overseas Workers Welfare Administration (OWWA), charged with providing welfare services. The OWWA assists the overseas workers and their families with a range of benefits:

- insurance for natural, accidental death and permanent disabilities;
- education scholarships for college level as well as for technical and vocational courses for the families of migrants;
- financial loans for the worker and the family members; and
- skills and competency upgrades to meet international norms for certain types of workers such as the seafarers.

Alongside these services, the OWWA officers implement onsite programs and activities designed to help migrant workers, especially women, cope with the problems of loneliness or homesickness. The Community Reach-Out Program (CROP), which includes workers' reorientation, consultation sessions, community organizing, leadership training and networking, is aimed at enhancing awareness, unity, cooperation and self-reliance among the Filipino communities and facilitating delivery of on-site services to migrant workers. The OWWA, likewise, looks after the families of the migrants left behind. Families of migrants are organized as self-help organizations at their localities, serving as support groups to families in-distress while the nuclear family member is working abroad.

Reintegration: Workers participating in the overseas employment program are given preparation to return to their families and communities at the Pre-Departure Orientation Seminar that they are required to attend as the final phase of the employment processing protocol. On their final briefing, there is a module that dwells on their responsibility to support the family, the prevailing system of remittances of wages, the value of savings, and preparation for their return. Options for the worker during and after completing his overseas employment are discussed.

The worksite preparation for the migrant's return includes a menu of alternatives of which they may avail - secondary skills acquisition through trainings and seminars offered at the Filipino Workers Resource Centers, competence upgrade via rating/board examinations conducted periodically, language training for adaptation to the worksite environ if the worker opts to remain for a longer period overseas and, finally, programs for livelihood and entrepreneurship that they may commence before or during their return to the local communities.

There are also financing plans available where they can draw venture capital for micro- and small-to-medium scale businesses at subsidized rates of interest to enable them to provide economic support to the family despite completed contract-migration. These same businesses also provide local employment generation to their communities.

Other Support Services. In parallel to the overseas employment program, other agencies of government provide support to the migrant while working abroad. Notably, they have the option of continuing membership in the Social Security System (SSS) operating under a defined pension scheme for old age. Aside from the regular SSS benefits, overseas Filipinos can also plan for their financial security through the SSS Flexi-fund Program, also adopted as the Provident Fund for overseas Filipino workers .

The National Home Mortgage Finance Corporation also opens their voluntary membership to permanent and temporary migrants to enable family members to avail themselves of the national shelter program through a preferential financing plan specifically designed for overseas Filipinos. Migrants are also provided special health maintenance coverage by the Philippine Health Insurance Corporation in a special enrollment plan. After 10 years of continuous membership while employed abroad, the overseas worker is provided subsidized medical care for the remaining years of his or her life.

In the entirety of overseas employment, the Filipino migrant is given protection by the government through ensuring that he or she is provided equitable terms and conditions of employment in a regulated recruitment structure; enjoys extended protection, assistance and welfare benefits while working abroad; and family members are provided the complementary benefits of the worker's employment by education and support/assistance services. Beyond the term of contractual employment, he or she is able to draw old-age pension, avail of a subsidized shelter program, and be covered with health maintenance services for ones remaining lifetime. This is all provided by the government to minimize the tensions of temporary migration and harmonize eventual reintegration into Philippine society, courtesy of a grateful nation.

All of these services require no less than 2 billion Filipino pesos annually, half of which comes from the national government, and the other half from an insurance fund paid into by workers or their employers. Together, these steps help ensure that workers get the best possible benefits from their overseas work and are able to maximize the positive effects of their work in another country.

This system of regulation, protection and reintegration is probably one of the few such systems in the world. It continues to be improved on not only because it is the politic thing to do, but because the state owes its workers no less. If migration is about managing tensions, these tensions operate not just in-country but outside as Filipinos seek to find better opportunities for themselves and their families. While some migrant workers eventually assume residency or permanence based on the rules of their host country, those who choose to return are brought back, either at the expense of their employers, as indicated in their contracts, or at the expense of the Philippine government. No Filipino in distress is turned away by its government.

Promoting Harmonious International Relations: The Philippine Response to the GCIM Recommendations

An overall assessment of current labor migration policies in the Philippines shows that the country has long been abiding by and adhering to the guiding principles set by the GCIM. A considerable amount of supporting evidence demonstrates how the segments of the GCIM framework are being implemented in the Philippine setting.

To further illustrate this point, it should be underscored that Filipinos are accorded the right to migrate out of choice. Only in three cases would the government restrict or impede international travel for Filipino nationals, that is, when the country of destination harbors threats to life, differences in public policy and morals. For instance, there is an imposed travel ban on Iraq as their current political situation would expose Filipino migrant workers to serious life-threatening risks. Filipinos are also prohibited from traveling to countries that lack labor policies which would safeguard migrant workers' rights and welfare, and where they would be rendered vulnerable to abuse or exploitation.

The Philippine government enthusiastically acknowledges the benefits of remittances received from Filipino migrant workers. Inward remittances have significantly contributed to national development and reduced poverty levels. As such, various government agencies have partnered with national and commercial banks to facilitate the safe and speedy transfer of remittance money from the Filipino migrant workers abroad to their beneficiaries in the Philippines. Now, Filipino migrant workers can open accounts with low minimum initial deposits, reduced remittance charges and no maintaining balance required.

At the micro level, the favorable effects of remittances cannot be overemphasized. These remittances have sent children or siblings to school, paid for a relative's medical needs, built houses, acquired appliances and amenities. In recognition of the Filipino migrant workers' key role in promoting economic and developmental prosperity in the Philippines, various government-initiated programs are continuously implemented and constantly improved to regulate policies relative to labor laws and standards.

To further address the issue of irregular migration, joint inter-agency efforts have also been intensified to combat illegal recruitment, human trafficking and prostitution. Increased vigilance is also exercised by airport police and the Coast Guard in order to thwart attempts to traffic people by passing through our country's exit points. The Labor Assistance Center also acts as a watch post in airports to avert trafficking of Filipino migrant workers.

The Philippine overseas employment model also ensures that returning migrant workers are easily reintegrated into Philippine society upon their return from their overseas stint. For instance, a migrant worker becomes eligible for a reintegration loan that can go as high as one million pesos, and even scholarships for migrant children and their spouses, organizing for support and assistance and entrepreneurship assistance become part of the support package.

Continuous efforts are also made to forge or upgrade bilateral or multilateral arrangements and agreements with host governments to ensure protection and welfare of Filipino migrant workers, observance of terms and conditions of the employment contracts, as well as provisions for further enhancement of the existing programs. The Philippine government regularly holds consultations with labor-receiving countries, international organizations and other stakeholders to improve labor migration systems worldwide.

Conclusion

This paper upholds the thesis that organized migration flows mitigate tensions between countries and societies. By deploying workers who are healthy, well-trained and properly documented, the host country's fears and reservations about accepting foreign workers are ultimately allayed and human security conflicts are kept at bay. With strong government support to assist Filipino nationals in properly integrating into their countries of destination and with a strong protection mechanism to safeguard their rights, Filipino migrant workers are spared from harrowing societal marginalization. Thus, social, political, cultural and even religious hostilities are averted.

The Philippine model, which pioneered the regulation-protection-reintegration system, has both stood the test of time and has also significantly increased the developmental benefits of temporary circular migration to the different actors involved in the employment process. Being the highly organized structure that it is, history has stood witness as it effectively precluded and combated a variety of conflicts which would have likely arose from a dysfunctional and problematic model.

Our dedicated mission to continually refine, and eventually perfect, our labor migration system in more ways than one has generated ripples of universal change. Thus, effective management of migration has been the Philippines' small and humble contribution to create and sustain an international community of peace, tolerance, good will and harmony and to support the achievement of the Millennium Development Goals.

Stock Estimate of Overseas Filipinos
As of December 2004

REGION / COUNTRY	PERMANENT	TEMPORARY	IRREGULAR	TOTAL
WORLD TOTAL	3,187,586	3,599,257	1,296,972	8,083,815
AFRICA	318	58,369	17,141	75,828
EGYPT	54	2,620	1,420	4,094
EQUATORIAL GUINEA	0	2,569	150	2,719
LIBYA	75	5,440	485	6,000
NIGERIA	18	11,750	586	12,354
OTHERS / UNSPECIFIED	171	35,990	14,500	50,661
ASIA, East & South	91,901	1,005,609	443,343	1,540,853
BRUNEI	26	21,762	1,700	23,488
HONGKONG	404	194,241	2,700	197,345
JAPAN	83,303	238,522	31,428	353,253
KOREA (South)	4,850	33,285	9,015	47,150
MACAU	56	17,391	1,000	18,447
MALAYSIA	313	52,337	300,000	352,650
SINGAPORE	152	64,337	72,000	136,489
TAIWAN	2,037	154,135	4,500	160,672
OTHERS / UNSPECIFIED	760	229,599	21,000	251,359
ASIA, West	2,312	1,449,031	112,750	1,564,093
BAHRAIN	64	33,154	3,500	36,718
ISRAEL	104	14,051	23,000	37,155
JORDAN	108	5,885	7,000	12,993
KUWAIT	93	80,196	11,500	91,789
LEBANON	19	28,318	6,100	34,437
OMAN	20	18,941	1,500	20,461
QATAR	13	57,345	1,000	58,358
SAUDI ARABIA	243	976,134	18,000	994,377
UAE	405	185,562	20,000	205,967
OTHERS / UNSPECIFIED	1,243	49,445	21,150	71,838
EUROPE	174,387	506,997	143,035	824,419
AUSTRIA	22,017	1,956	2,000	25,973
BELGIUM	3,583	3,484	5,533	12,600
FRANCE	1,098	4,866	26,121	32,085
GERMANY	42,882	8,346	4,400	55,628
GREECE	88	17,058	8,000	25,146
ITALY	4,934	85,527	48,000	138,461
NETHERLANDS	10,421	2,920	2,000	15,341
SPAIN	16,332	6,960	2,000	25,292

SWITZERLAND	922	7,025	6,700	14,647
UNITED KINGDOM	52,500	56,341	7,481	116,322
OTHERS / UNSPECIFIED	19,610	312,514	30,800	362,924

REGION / COUNTRY	PERMANENT	TEMPORARY	IRREGULAR	TOTAL
AMERICAS / TRUST TERRITORIES	2,689,722	292,892	549,725	3,532,339
CANADA	369,225	32,766	2,975	404,966
UNITED STATES	2,271,933	101,249	350,000	2,723,182
CNMI	1,288	16,753	1,250	19,291
GUAM	45,968	1,800	500	48,268
OTHERS / UNSPECIFIED	1,308	140,324	195,000	336,632
OCEANIA	228,946	57,357	30,978	317,281
AUSTRALIA	211,664	930	2,900	215,494
NEW ZEALAND	17,182	307	120	17,609
PALAU	5	3,702	400	4,107
PAPUA NEW GUINEA	64	5,030	7,339	12,433
OTHERS / UNSPECIFIED	31	47,388	20,219	67,638
SEABASED WORKERS		229,002		229,002

Prepared by the Commission on Filipinos Overseas from CFO, DFA, POEA and other sources covering 194 countries / territories.

Permanent - Immigrants or legal permanent residents abroad whose stay do not depend on work contracts.

Temporary - Persons whose stay overseas is employment related, and who are expected to return at the end of their work contracts.

Irregular - Those not properly documented or without valid residence or work permits, or who are overstaying in a foreign country.

References

Books

Migration in an interconnected world: New directions for action
Report of the Global Commission on International Migration
Switzerland, 2005

Websites

Department of Labor and Employment
http://www.dole.gov.ph

Overseas Workers' Welfare Administration
http://www.owwa.gov.ph

Philippine Overseas Employment Administration
http://www.poea.gov.ph

Bangko Sentral ng Pilipinas (Central Bank of the Philippines)
http://www.bsp.gov.ph

National Statistical Coordination Board
http://www.nscb.gov.ph

Litho in United Nations, New York, United Nations publication
07-66423—April 2008—2,840 Sales No. E.08.II.H.3
ISBN 978-92-1-123175-5 ST/ESA/PAD/SER.E/116